DAMAGED
BONDS

DAMAGED BONDS

Michael Eigen

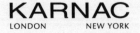
KARNAC
LONDON   NEW YORK

First published in 2001 by
H. Karnac (Books) Ltd.
6 Pembroke Buildings, London NW10 6RE

A subsidiary of Other Press LLC, New York

British Library Cataloguing in Publication Data

A C.I.P. for this book is available from the British Library

ISBN 1 85575 256 5

10 9 8 7 6 5 4 3 2 1

Edited, designed, and produced by Communication Crafts
Printed and bound in Great Britain by Biddles Ltd, *www.biddles.co.uk*

www.karnacbooks.com

An overheard conversation:

"The human heart is warped, gnarled, joyous."

"Yes, but we give it our best shot, no?"

"We want to. We're so strange. Even aliveness is a discovery."

"We discover the damage we grow in, that grows in us."

"Why not make that our dedication? To damaged bonds."

"Damaged, damaging, sometimes also generative."

"To generative bonds, then?"

"It sounds so circular."

"Well, then, to moments the circle opens."

CONTENTS

PART TWO
Work in the trenches

PREFACE

It is hard to believe that I have been working as a psychotherapist for forty years. I have seen many fashions come and go and some of them endure. One of my greatest debts is to the therapy field itself, for providing a world, a milieu, a place that enabled me to use myself in ways that made a difference in many lives, usually for the better. At the same time, I could continue my lifelong research on myself, banging my head against edges of my own psychic universe, sometimes finding useful and precious openings.

In the early 1960s I began to work as a therapist for schizophrenic children, then worked with adults and children in psychoanalytic psychotherapy, eventually becoming certified as a psychologist and psychoanalyst. In the 1970s I began publishing, sharing soundings from worlds I was discovering—work in the trenches. As the decades went on, I absorbed many influences—Freud, Jung, Adler, Fromm, Kohut, existentialism, gestalt psychology, humanism, body therapies, British and French psychoanalysis, and much creative work in my own country, very alive in ferment today. I have loved all these branches of depth psychology and more. They nourished me and gave me tools with which to go further with myself and others. They opened worlds of experience and meaning.

There are not many writers I read on a weekly or monthly basis. Three of them are Bion, Winnicott, and Lacan. The first two are especially important as background supports of this book. Bion and Winnicott overlap in many ways. They are both concerned with madness in its destructive and creative aspects. And they are both concerned with damage to self or personality and with our capacity to live. Both feel that our sense of aliveness has a rough time and can cause damage as well as get damaged. It can be poisoned and poisonous and become numb as life continues. Yet in each of these authors there is a deep faith or sense that generative processes are ubiquitous if they can be given a chance. Aliveness needs support and practice to fare well, to reach workable combinations of decency and creativeness.

It is one of life's chilling characteristics that bonds that nourish also damage. We are formed and malformed at the same time. In an earlier work, *Toxic Nourishment* (1999), I explored ways that emotional nourishment and toxins are fused. *Damaged Bonds* complements and adds to this, by encouraging us to look at and face, as we can, how we wound and are wounded by the bonds we need to live. It is, perhaps, part of life's oddity that doing so, to the extent we are able, brings its own kind of joy. It is even sometimes (far from always) true that the more severe the damage, the more intense the joy.

Both Winnicott and Bion place a lot on dreaming. Both feel that dreaming plays an important role in feeling alive, and that linking dreaming with waking is part of what makes life feel like life. Winnicott differs from Bion by spending more time on what things are like when they go well. But he depicts the sinking and dying of feeling and being when things do not go well enough. Nevertheless, no author I know depicts what happens in us when things go wrong in as close a way as does Bion. One of his points of emphasis is that our dream-work can get damaged, and when it does, our capacity to digest and process mental and emotional food is injured.

It is an underlying assumption of this book that the therapy bond (both damaged/damaging and generative) helps support dream-work and connections between dream reality and everyday waking activities. It is thus, also, our hope that therapy helps to improve psychic digestion. At a minimum, we suspect that it will help us to learn something about our relationship to emotional processes, so that we become better partners to ourselves and others. This is a faith that therapy and life is always testing—although I do not like distinguishing between therapy and life. Therapy is a form life takes—not only a way life tries to repair and detoxify itself, but also an attempt at creating new life, including qualities and uses of bonds with possibilities that may take lifetimes to discover.

There is an overlap between themes in this book and religion, art, and literature. Explorations of soul damage, survival, and regeneration take many forms. Therapy is a kind of slow-motion action painting with emotions and thoughts within and between people. The taste and feel or quality of personal presence is at stake. In therapy we have a chance to slow things down, to chew on moments of injury/regeneration, and to taste and partly digest what ordinarily sweeps us along. We get a chance to test out, absorb, and work with what we fear (often rightly so) may be annihilating about life-giving bonds. An ancient mystery renewed in therapy involves, reciprocally, learning how undergoing certain forms of annihilation can add to life.

ACKNOWLEDGEMENTS

My thanks to the National Psychological Association for Psychoanalysis and the New York University Postdoctoral Program in Psychotherapy and Psychoanalysis for an opportunity to teach and supervise and keep in touch with a variety of excellent students and colleagues with complementary and conflicting viewpoints. It is important to be able to situate what one is doing in a broader horizon, learn what one can, yet dig into areas one is led to. Thanks to Rick Burnett and Jamaica Hospital, Judith Young and the Institute for Expressive Analysis, Ross Skelton and the European Association of Psychotherapy in conjunction with the Irish Council for Psychotherapy, Marvin Lifschitz and the Westchester Institute for Training in Psychotherapy and Psychoanalysis, Lew Aron, Anthony Molino, Judith Newman, Joseph Reppen, Joseph Bobrow, and Annie Sweetnam for asking me to talk or write or be included in collections of writings. Many thanks for long-time good wishes from Mark Epstein, Jessica Benjamin, Jeff Eaton, James Grotstein, Otto Weininger, Christopher Bollas, Adam Phillips, Emmanuel Ghent, Art Robbins, and Edward Emery.

A new kind of acknowledgement involves the Internet. For the past several years, I have interacted with the Bion site run by Silvio Merciai, and I have been grateful to have such a resource. On Dr Merciai's site, I have benefited from comments by Paulo Sandler, Roberto Olsner, and many others. Thanks to Robert Young for consistent help and to Cheryl Martin for putting my work on her site, *Psychematters*. Email resources have been mind-boggling, making it possible to be quickly in touch with people I would otherwise never have known.

I have been doing therapy longer than I have been married, but without my family—Betty, David, and Jacob—my books would not have been written. Papers and articles, yes, but not books. The sustained intensity and nervous energy that goes into a book can drive one crazy, if one does not drive one's family crazy instead.

Thanks to Graham Sleight for accepting this book at Karnac and for his helpful, literate comments and associations, a number of which I integrated into the text. I like to think that Mr Sleight's love of music has something to do with his interest in my work. I failed to acknowledge Communication Crafts for work done on my previous book with Karnac Books, *Toxic Nourishment*, and so have a chance to double the thanks now. I hope *Damaged Bonds* and *Toxic Nourishment* will be read together—sister books, two images or slices of omnipresent reality.

A number of these chapters grew out of the private seminar I have been giving on Bion, Winnicott, and Lacan. The seminar has been going for 25 years or more and has been a wonderful outlet and stimulus and support—a kind of therapy launching-pad. In the seminar we can talk and share our visions and sense of what we do and fail to do. We can approach the psychic damage that bonds inflict, knowing that there is group support (generative bond) to try to process some of this damage. Often the damage becomes part of the group—threatens to overwhelm. As best we can, we hold hands, let go of hands, leap, and tell each other what we find.

My patients are my main resource in this work, and there is no way I can give them what they give me. I have taken precautions to preserve their anonymity and in many instances sought permission to use what I have written. People who come to see me know that I am a writer, but they may also expect a certain care in what I write. I try to be true to the soul of therapy, let the latter speak, yet a certain amount of disguise is necessary.

My own insides speak through my patients. The samplings of work offered here are hot off the psyche. If it is a truism that I am helped by patients, it is also true that I am helped by writing. Dream-work that goes into helping another person goes into writing about trying to help too, and if the work is successful, help spreads.

For the sake of simplicity and to make the text easier to read, the author has used the masculine pronoun throughout for all unspecified therapists and patients.

DAMAGED
BONDS

"These shattered bonds . . . look, the scattered pieces turn into sparks of light. Is that possible?"

"No. They are sharp pieces of glass scraping what is left of soul."

Michael Eigen

—Salvation by way of complete destruction?

—There is no other way.

Flann O'Brien

"O'Brien is quite mad, you know. Complete destruction—that's idealism. Most are stuck somewhere partly destroyed. They've no suspicion there's a knack to letting destruction do good work. They tense up, protect themselves, find ways of getting through. They miss out."

"But doesn't one need to dream destruction?"

"We must. We do. But will we find a way to let this dreaming do its work?"

Michael Eigen

"I'm so miserable since you left me/It's a lot like having you around."

Country Song Joke

Introduction

Whe think of damaged bonds, we think of ties to
one another, parent–baby bonding, links to self, other,
universe. No one escapes damage to these bonds or to
one's linking capacity. Yet we live with our damaged relational
capacity and sometimes live well. We make the best of damaged
selves with a mixture of pushing past, ignoring, transcending, and
trying to heal our sense of injury.

It may be that psychological damage is an intrinsic part of
bonding processes, just as a certain amount of physical damage is a
natural part of birthing. We take for granted violence attached to
hatching processes, but we play down the role of violence and loss
in forging links. We are damaged by bonds that give us life, disabled by connections that help us to grow, succoured by damaging
processes. Sometimes the damage that is part of growth processes
takes centre stage, and one becomes obsessed with damage rather
than throwing oneself into life. A side effect of larger processes
becomes consuming.

On the other hand, much of social life is premised on the assumption that we do not damage each other when we say hello and

chat or share experiences. We make believe that things are better than they are for the sake of what is gained. Unfortunately, the habit of ignoring damage increases our inability to work with damage when the latter requires attention. We move back and forth between these extremes, learning to work with consequences of damaging processes when necessary, looking away nimbly when a lighter touch is better.

Therapy is in the paradoxical position of helping people to live less damaged/damaging lives while aware that any human interaction has damaging aspects. It would be nice to think that therapy is self-healing, that it transcends or mends the damage it inflicts as it helps. Some feel the answer to the damaging aspects of therapy is more therapy, and perhaps this is one reason why therapy can be interminable—it is ever trying to catch up to, undo, or go beyond the harm it does as it helps.

It may be that therapy never heals all the damage it causes but passes it on to the great cauldron of life, which the patient is more ready to live. Yet discussion in detail of the ways we damage each other by the bonds we need adds to our appreciation of life's texture, limits, and possibilities.

Damage inflicted when personality is forming can reach unconscious substructures that are necessary to support psychic life. Processes such as Freud described as "dream-work" help to digest the impact of events and play a role in metabolizing affects. If dream-work is damaged, it is difficult for emotional damage to right itself. If, so to speak, the "apparatus" that processes and transforms affect is damaged, a person's relationship to what is bothering him is self-defeating.

Therapy helps dream-work to function. To a certain extent, the therapist becomes an auxiliary dream processor, giving the patient the support needed to enable the growth of primary process work. Primary process helps to initiate emotional digestion and is, among other things, concerned with catastrophic impacts. As chapters one to four suggest, dream-work or primary process can be damaged by the damage it tries to work with, and the therapist provides and helps to stimulate new possibilities for emotional processing.

Much of dream-work is concerned with damage done to personality. As implied above, dream-work tries to process damage done to it. Damaged dream-work works with damaged bonds.

Therapy takes this state of affairs seriously and gives the self a chance to signal what it feels is wrong. A therapist may or may not get the message, but he tries to stay with the situation until it begins to reach him. To talk about reaching the patient before the therapist is reached can be premature. The therapist speaks from a place he is touched, which includes his own incomplete, ongoing bonding process, with its incessant dream-work.

Inability to process emotional life can make a person feel he is lacking in some capacity. He may not make the connection between damaged bonds and damaged dream-work but simply feel that something is wrong—not working right. He may not have a clue that problems with emotional digestion help to maintain a larger sense of disability.

In chapter one, "Damaged Bonds", I introduce the notion that developing a working emotional sense of oneself involves more than "will" or "choice". I appeal to implicit worlds of permeability between people. Yes, "will" and "choice" are important, and personality forms around them. But often they take the place of emotional flow. Where the latter is lacking, self congeals and becomes obsessed with will and choices.

To say this is not to overthrow any notion of responsibility in favour of a pessimistic determinism. It is simply to open up the flow more between us, our awareness of what we do to each other moment by moment, our mutual impacts. We set in motion waves of impacts, or, rather, find ourselves immersed in fields of impacts already in progress. To pay attention to how some of these impacts feel and how these feelings change as we attend to them is no small order. We often tend to act as if we know what we feel before we give our feelings a chance to develop.

There is a dimension deeper than will and more interesting. How we feel in the presence of another human being opens worlds of experiencing to which will and choice cannot do justice. We overemphasize the roles of control, desire, and mastery as a way of avoiding open seas of relationship and never-ending nuances of being.

The cases of "Lena", "Chris", and "Laura" (chapter one) introduce themes we all face. Tensions between opening and closing, thawing and tightening are part of the rise and ebb and swirl of feelings that create the colour of a moment—expressions on the face of one's life. There are times to get into one's pain, times to let pain go. In most cases, in this book, we go deeper into the pain of life; but in doing so, our ability to see what is there grows more inclusive, and the scope of experiencing becomes more subtle.

It takes a great deal to attend to the state of self, the state of a moment, and transformations of states over time. It is not a capacity that can compete with the will to power and money. It may be easier to make millions of dollars than to follow complex transformations of feelings moment to moment. Yet individuals have, from time to time, devoted themselves to tasting and probing states of being in the hope of seeing what is there. It is a capacity we intermittently dip into, explore, exploit. It involves a taste for subjectivity—a taste that, one or another way, has been valued. In the end, it involves a most precious capacity: our very sense of what it feels like to be alive, to be a person, a conscious/unconscious being.

The taste is not always good. As a therapist, it is necessary to go ever deeper into strangulated states—not only to observe, but to feel the closing-in on oneself, collapsing, enduring mutilation, becoming aware of rotten, ruptured areas of one's own life. One sees areas of self or personality or being ravaged by trauma. At times, the damage takes on a life of its own, as if once begun, it becomes self-perpetuating. But often one finds damage to self tied to embedded damaged objects that are now part of self. It is not possible to remove the damage to self by removing the damaged object (e.g. residues of a depressed or psychotic or abusive parent): the damage is done. But one can help a person to open new channels to process the damage, enabling new states of self to evolve.

I have become convinced that much of what happens in therapy, often what is most important, is non-verbal—permanently outside the reach of words. This in no way minimizes the use of words. There are people who must storm the gates with words, try to say everything. Sometimes they take words or words take them over the edge, opening paths of experience. Words do lead to new aspects of reality. But in most therapeutic work, there is a tone or atmosphere or "feel" in the room that is more important. Words, after all, do not merely involve the exchange of information—they are part of the "exchange" of states of being.

There is an "osmotic" aspect to therapy that must not be overlooked. People are sensitive and feel each other's impacts but often

do not know what to do with them. A therapist is a kind of special-
ist in letting the other in, feeling the impact of the other, staying
with images and thoughts to which the feel of the other gives rise.
A patient not only senses the therapist, but senses how he affects
the therapist. What does a therapist do with this impact? To what
extent can he let it build? Where will it take him?

The patient, in a way, reads himself in the therapist's being and
vice versa. There are unspoken dramas in every human interaction.
Is there room for me in another's feeling life? To what extent must
I short-circuit myself in order to communicate at all? Where do
feeling exchanges start? How far can they go? So much goes on
moment to moment once we tune into it—how much of ourselves
and each other can we endure or enjoy? How much and in what
ways dare we let ourselves and each other in? A relationship devoted to how we enable and block experiencing ourselves and each
other creates a bond devoted to processing bonding damage and
the ways we short-circuit life-giving feelings.

Damaged bonds and damaged dream-work go together. In part
one—the first four chapters—Bion's writings on damaged dream-
work are explored. Many dreams are concerned with trying to
process wounds to our psychic digestive system. Wounded dream-
work tries to cure itself. It tries to heal or depict its injured state. It
tries to get at the damaged bonds that warp, block, or immobilize
its efforts. It does the best it can on its own but often can do a little
better with a helping hand.

Bion feels that dreams cannot do their dreaming work if what
they are compelled to do is digest a state of affairs that damages
digestion or, in effect, dream a damaging object that dream-work
cannot put together. Bion depicts this object as a murderous superego that is too frightening for the psyche to assemble. He calls
attention to a fright that stops psychic functioning in basic ways,
particularly with regard to processing emotional life. The capacity
for emotional nourishment keeps getting wounded, and the
wounding process, like Medusa or God, stymies the psyche's attempts to see and digest it.

Part two consists of six chapters depicting stymied states and
shifts they undergo—or fail to undergo. Whether implicitly or ex-
plicitly, these chapters concern dramas revolving around difficulties in psychic digestion and clinical work in the trenches. Bion

feels that dream-work goes on (or fails) continuously, awake or asleep. We keep trying to process bits of reality, bits of joy and trauma. Much therapy goes on inside damaged bonds, where the dream tries to resuscitate itself and do its job. There is a drive to unite emotional nourishment with emotional truth, to touch facts of life, to taste the real. That dream is part of our reality adds to the wonder of who we are and the challenge of learning to use our capacities. Successful dream-work often goes on invisibly, seemingly dissolving itself as it goes. Very like the osmotic aspect of therapy, no one may know it is there, and the individual may wonder how he got better.

The last chapter is autobiographical, portraying parts of the dream of my life as actually lived. In a way, this whole book is a kind of dream trying to process a bit of the unprocessable, imaging damage we need to see. It is part of the attempt each one of us makes to see God/Medusa and live.

PART ONE

DAMAGED BONDS— DAMAGED DREAMS

CHAPTER ONE

Damaged bonds

T he amazing changes human beings go through moment to moment throughout a day inspire awe. It is glorious when these shifts bring variations in happiness. But many are variants of misery. I have asked people whether they think there is pain at ecstasy's centre, and many said yes. Yet, the reverse makes them uncomfortable: they do not like to think that there is ecstasy in pain. Yet pleasure/pain and agony/ecstasy ever blend, as the sensation–feeling kaleidoscope they are part of turns and turns.

When one thinks of invincibility, one thinks less of feelings and sensations than of will: invincible will. Years of clinical work have brought me face to face with the grisly fact that people who seem overwhelmed with every shift of mood and situation, who complain that they have no will of their own and are always giving in to others, are, nevertheless, gripped by an unbudgeable will that cannot let go. This *will* may play a role in enabling survival, but often it puts life on hold. Too often it becomes empty will, feeding its own existence without giving the individual much in the way of nourishment.

Will is generally associated with positive values. It is good to have a will of one's own, pursue one's course, stand up for oneself in the face of other wills. Will goes along with being an active agent, making one's way in life. To have free will means to have a capacity for choice. Often will is associated with power, mastery, ambition, self-esteem. In an expansive life, will adds to the colour, richness, and fullness of living.

But what of the life that undergoes successive contractions, until what is left is not much more than a strangulated knot?—a will that tightens around itself like a fist that cannot open . . . and keeps tightening, trapped by its own density, becoming like a black hole, denser and darker as time goes on (for the "black hole" image in therapeutic work, see Eigen, 1999; Grotstein, 1990a, 1990b; Tustin, 1981).

"Lena"

In a recent session, Lena recognized a baffling duality. She was complaining about the way she changes, depending on the person she is with: "I can't bear being so adaptable, a regular Zellig (Woody Allen's chameleon character who changes into the person he is with). I can't hold my own. I become frightened, quivering, slavish. I go along, agree. Yet there's something unreachable in me, hidden. I'm changeable like weather, always worrying. But I know there is something unmoved, unyielding, a tiny island no one can find."

Lena described a kind of emotion–sensation swirl stained by worry around an impenetrable point. She felt that she was an aberrant instance of plasticity/persistence, both permeable and impenetrable in the extreme. Her emotional reactivity made her feel slavish, while a still, small point of will rendered her unconquerable, if not masterful. At the same time, Lena complained about being grotesque. It was not her emotional lability or diffusion that made her feel this way, but something severe, merciless, inhuman about the untouchable sliver of will. While seemingly an island of safety, this shrunken bit of will made Lena feel like a monster. Her diffuse emotionality made her feel more human. She was less afraid that God would blast her for hysterical catastrophizing than point to the grain of will that remained outside life.

For many years, this hardened point of will played a role in Lena's survival. It helped to calculate possibilities/probabilities, counselled when to hide or come out, take this or that course. Will and judgement were welded together. As suggested above, all the compliance in the world could not force will to give in. When I first began to notice it, I could not tell if it was a sane point of refuge in the storm or an all-seeing madness contracting towards invisibility.

As time went on, will seemed less interested in Lena's survival than in its own.[1] As Lena got better, the will that could get through anything seemed bent against a fuller life. Perhaps it had become used to its contracted state and felt thawing out or expansion a threat. It gripped Lena's growing self like a dying hand clutches the flesh of the living. A once indomitable will fragment feared being left behind, as if Lena no longer needed it. What would happen if she outgrew it?

States of mind serving well at one point are hindrances at another. The contracted ball of survival–will that saw Lena through kept her coiled, stopped her from opening. She let her husband and friends in only so far, then snapped shut. When she tried to let herself in, the steel ball of will closed. Cold judgement beset by panic took the place of opening, against wishes of a growing, fuller self. The contracted ball of will often had a malignant aspect. Friends were judged by faults, life was reduced to whatever was wrong with it. Will made Lena suspicious. Little escaped its evil eye, clinging beyond its time.

Can personality grow around a core of contracted will? Can will evolve with personality? Must contractions relied on in worse

---

[1] It almost seems as if bits of psychic life take on lives of their own, not only as objects but as subjects. In literature this theme has been objectified as a created monster or machine turning against its maker. Jung wrote of psychic archipelagos, with somatopsychic nuclei and concerns. Dissociations/splits never ceased exercising Freud (see Eigen, 1986, for discussions of differing ways Freud and Jung approached subjective multiplicity). Bion (e.g. 1991, pp. 83–84) repeatedly noted how psychic formations, successful in one context, multiplied problems in another.

conditions poison development when growth is possible? Lena was tyrannized by what saved her, yet she recognized that it was time to move on, if she could.

Holes and violence: "Chris"

Some individuals try to fill the gap between will and feelings with violence—in Chris's case, with violent dreams and fantasies. Chris dreamt of *a woman with a hole in her head. She was dying, blood on the floor.* Chris was obsessed with rape. He avidly followed news reports of rape, he read all he could.

How did his woman get a hole in her head? From her father's violent fucking or fantasy fucking? From Chris's rape wishes? Was the dream depicting a damaged primary object, something wrong from the outset? Did the dream defend against and depreciate Woman by displacing a hole upwards and making her brain dead? Is Woman represented as dead because she is too alive? Is such extreme reversal (down ↔ up, aliveness ↔ deadness) needed to ward off aliveness, chaos, hysteria? Did the dream portray environmental deficiency that scarred Chris's upbringing? Did it depict psychological rape, his death, his brain hole, his fear of life?

Whatever the specifics may be, something is terribly wrong. Chris's dream gives voice to violent damage. Many patients say: "There is something wrong with me. I've always known it. Something was wrong from the beginning." Here the hole in life is depicted in a dying woman's head. Imagine growing up with a woman perceived in this way: a damaged parent, ever haemorrhaging, near brain-death.

"Whatever I did caused Mom pain. She bled with pain. I couldn't breathe without hurting her."

Here was a real/fantasy mother concerned more with her own pain than with her child's. The balance between sensing one's own and the other's pain is always in jeopardy, and getting stuck in either direction is always a possibility.

Rape is fury at maternal damage, an act of revenge. One damages the damaged one, tries to take control over the brutal facts. Rape, too, tries to repair the damage. One tries to rape mother into life, make her whole, fix her. Of course, there is a matter of power—one tries to get power over what made one feel powerless, rape in return for feeling raped or neglected. Opposites are equals in mad logic—in addition to Freud, I am thinking of Bion's equivalencies (1992, p. 22) and Matte-Blanco's (1975, 1988) symmetrical unconscious, as well as much else written on unconscious life.

"I thought she'd like it." Substitute *me* for *it*. One wants a response and hopes for more than one gets. In the unconscious of the rapist there is an imaginary Whole Person loving a Whole Person. The act of rape aims at love. "I feel loved"—as if love, violation, and hate were equivalent. It is difficult to concede being lost in a realm where damage begets damage. Rape fails in its Pygmalion task. It does not repair or create the object or self but for moments yields illusory wholeness that hides the grisly fact that real work one needs to do is beyond ability.

Chris is in therapy and can talk about damage and failed repair. He will not rape anyone. Rape is his fantasy only, but the damage is real. He was wounded by parental rages, chaos, neglect, and deadness when his personality was forming, and he grew as he could. Warps result from poisons one deals with.

Rape is a way to feel self, to create and blur distinctions between self and other—part of a fantasy of repair or creation. The paradox is blood-curdling. A damaging act is, in part, connected with a wish for reparation. One repairs by inflicting damage. One heals by injuring. One tries to get what one needs from an object—but the getting is an act of partial annihilation.

Part for whole: partial annihilation substitutes for total annihilation. Rape and murder *can* go together. But in Chris's case, raper/rapist survive the violent act. Part of the power of the scene is that *survival occurs against a background dread of total annihilation.*

An irony for Chris is that relationships are pale and lost if they are not mean and harmful. He breaks up with women who are not mean enough or who cannot support his meanness. Yet he is too nice to be too mean and too sensitive to take much meanness, so he breaks with lovers if meanness mounts. Relationships do not feel real without damage and are unbearable with damage. Perhaps breaking up is the only safe way to feel damage—damage at a distance. In Chris's life, relationships break as they are forming. Something is always on the verge of breaking, beginning to break, actually breaking, and, finally, broken. The tear, the rip, the break feels real—for a time.

One might suppose that raping/breaking is what goes on in Chris's soul, with a magical sense that wounds are healed by being addicted to them. What keeps Chris riveted to this position, forever trying/failing? One factor is more primary object damage than he can repair, in a kind of "sorcerer's apprentice" situation: the more damage he tries to fix, the more he finds. The O of his life is too damaged for him to get the response he needs. Perhaps there are cases in which one can rape O into responding. [Bion's O (1965, 1970; Eigen, 1998) is a notation for "ultimate reality", including core emotional reality (realities) of a person's life.] But this does not work for Chris. The damage is too extensive from the beginning. His mind produces fantasies that go around in circles, get nowhere, reflecting and masking an impermeable emotional reality that is nearly beyond reach.

There is mad, compulsive will in Chris's rape fantasies. In reality, it makes a difference whether one is victim or perpetrator. In the mad unconscious, these differences wash out. Active/passive meld, become equivalent. Energy is more primary than evanescent forms it takes. In Chris's case, rape compresses a sense of power/powerlessness, mastery/helplessness, wounding/wounded. Victim and perpetrator become configurations for aggressive energy to circulate in variable keys. Rape as an image of trauma—part of what being a baby felt like. Injury/dread/fury congeal and, in Chris's case, crystallize, several times removed, as obsession with violation: his and parental power/powerlessness, his and parental damaged/damaging states.

Rape attempts to unite pleasure with injury—a warped, triumphant ecstasy of wholeness amidst abject pain. The pain of the victim is an important ingredient for the perpetrator's ecstasy of power. In the deep unconscious, the victim is oneself as well as object of revenge. The victim is an emblem of the pain of life, all that one endures, the mutilated self. It is as if, for a moment, one becomes the master of pain, master of the sense of injury. At the same time, one *is* the injured party once removed, one *is* the pain one feels in the other's body, voice, face. The inflictor is mesmerized by soul damage pinned, like a butterfly, in the skin of the other.

The image of rape gives to more generalized damage "a local habitation and a name". Chris grew up in a sea of injury—pain everywhere. The damage he suffered was disorganized, inchoate, immense. To compress it into an obsession with rape is an attempt to place boundaries on the damage. In Chris's case, the compression works only partly, as deep pain wreaks havoc in many ways, including somatic symptoms, work and relational problems, variable anxieties, depressing rigidities. Nevertheless, his obsession provides moments of imaginary triumph amidst pervasive pain, a sense of possibility in the face of soul damage. The fact that Chris clings to therapy while ever threatening to leave suggests that he is determined to give himself a chance. (He has been in therapy for four years—a long time for some, but in the face of the damage Chris works with, a bare, if significant, beginning.) Here will—a besieged, reduced, enduring will to live—points him towards help, although it remains to be seen what help is possible.

Damaged bonds: "Laura"

Recently, Laura told me that she married her husband, "Will", because they were damaged in ways that fitted together. They stayed together for their entire adult lives, and their damaged bond deepened. Now she could look back at all they had gone through and feel their bond a blessing, part of what gave life substance. It had not always been that way.

When they were young, they had bonded together to escape their families. They were freedom for each other, a way into life. Family life was mean and suffocating. Laura and Will enjoyed each other. They did everything together. But as time went on, the mean and suffocating feeling they escaped began to grow between them. Their first nourishing years turned into years of hellish nourishment—then just hell.

The damage characterizing family ties caught up with them. At this juncture, many couples flee each other to search for the free, uncontaminated feeling once more. Separation was a pressing option for Laura and Will for many years, but their attempts to break up failed. Neither knew why they stayed together, although Laura secretly sensed that they would weather it. Many years of therapy helped.

Laura felt crushed by an egocentric, rejecting mother. She found a little warmth from a more caring but distant, respectful father. Laura knew she was injured by her mother's coarse, bullying ways. The latter's petty scorn tore her down from the beginning. It took years to digest the fact that warmth hurt too. Her mother intermittently poured her whole noxious force through whatever random warmth she managed. Her father's warmth was not enough to protect Laura in daily life. It amounted to a tease of what might have been, had he been available.

It is one thing to be wounded by cruelty and neglect. It is even worse if the warmth one chances on tantalizes and poisons. For Laura, primary sources of nourishment were damaged and damaging. She did her best to live off damaged bonds and form what connection to life she could. To be wounded by nourishment can leave one shaken for life (Eigen, 1999).

Poisons in her upbringing permeated her marriage. Her husband put her down. His oblivious sense of male superiority felt like her mother's scorn. Laura would ruefully "joke" that Will combined the worst of her parents: mother's contemptuous insensitivity and father's distance. Through the worst, she knew that Will was not as poisonous as her mother. But she felt as disregarded, unseen, unheard. She did not feel that she could get through to Will, or that it would make any difference if she could. She felt he was unchangeable, thoughtless, and determined to be on top at her expense. Living with him was a disaster. He did not seem able to catch on to himself.

Years of hell began to lift somewhat when Will tried to listen to her. He began hearing her complain that he could not hear her. She kept hammering the point home that he was unable to listen, that he did not let anything in. It took years for him to notice *that* much, still light-years from being open to her perspective. Yet Laura noticed hints of influence. There were times he understood her for moments before the glimmer faded—a little like being frustrated by her father's hints of warmth. Now you see it, now you don't. Nothing to see you through on a daily basis.

Laura would not settle for crumbs. She kept fighting, in her stubborn way. For years, she felt she had given up. Yet something in her would not give up. Will could not make an about-face, but something happened. Laura felt that Will was beginning to notice that he was living with someone else—someone with her own mind and preferences, someone he had to take into account. Tastes of reciprocity were not as impossible as they had once seemed. The easy oneness of their early years was not possible, since it had been built on Laura's unconscious conformity with Will. But hints of new types of meeting appeared. It was more than getting past the hell of being antagonists and constantly lobbying for incompatible interests. They began to feel each other's aliveness, each other's subjectivity. Aloneness is satisfied not by oneness, but by the fact that someone else is there. Shareable moments become linked with a sense of coming through something together.

One day Laura startled me by saying that she sensed things would work from the outset: "I knew when I married Will that our getting along was based on suppressing myself. I went along with it because I knew that's the way it had to be at the time. I traded off something horrible [family life] for something that would become horrible, but was good at the time. I knew we'd have to go through hell. I knew we could break up, that I would hate him, that life would be unbearable. I could see in him a lot of what I was trying to get away from. I knew that from the beginning and hid it from myself.

"I had faith, a feeling, a sense that Will was not *just* like my family. Common traits, but not *just* the same. The thing in him I loved is still there. I don't just hate him. When I feel *him*, his *life*, I feel good inside too. Sometimes hate seems deeper, but good feeling comes back. A deep bond inside. A crazy bond maybe. Our crazy families are in it. But there's also life. I knew he couldn't change the way I wanted exactly. But we would change. We wouldn't lose to the worst.

"The hells now seem part of something bigger. Our bond absorbs hell and gives weight, solidity, realness to life. I picked someone to go through something bad, to reach bad things that were part of me. Someone who could get through it with me. Someone I could *be* with. I sensed it from the beginning."

For Laura, Will helped to give life its taste and *vice versa*. They, in part, tasted life through each other. Will and Laura became part of each other's psychic bodies. A crazy life-taking, life-giving bond crystallizes, becomes tenacious, goes through partial changes. Damaged/damaging selves deposit damage in damaged/damaging bonds that partly find ways to heal, partly make things good. Laura's bond with Will found circuitous ways into the goodness of life through the wisdom of pain. Laura sensed a will to come through in the background of her being—a persistent, tenacious will that would not let go. She *would* come through—with a lot of help. Yet not all Lauras come through.

The will to come through: "Chris"

Chris could not encode his damage in a self-healing bond. For him, damage undid bonds as they formed. His relationship to therapy was fragile and brittle. His contracted will held on tightly, but emotional flow through it was greatly reduced. His focus on rape imagery substituted intensity in a highly specialized mould for richness, variation, flow.

His damaged self was hungry for healing but embedded in a damaged primary object that did not heal. He reached for healing but opposing forces were strong. Was there more life in the negative force, more life in illness than in therapy? Could therapy offer an alternative attachment? Perhaps only a therapy mad or ill enough could stand a chance.

A damaged/damaging primary object is buried deep in the self, out of reach. A body may blacken and die where blood cannot circulate; a wound cannot heal without sufficient blood flow. The damaged/damaging object, like a mad, dumb tick, burrows to a place beyond blood flow. Cut off from nourishment, it blackens and may never be able to be part of life again.

Still, something of the patient may be able to be part of life. Chris has not totally given up, but he lacks Laura's will to come through. His resolve repeatedly crumbles when a bond begins to form. He cannot help it. He runs away. Perhaps running away is part of his resolve—a resolve that works in reverse, a negative resolve. A will *not* to come through as a means of "survival", as if he only trusts what protects him from life, defences against healing, as if healing would be annihilating. Running away from life is the way he lives. Every bond signals disaster, and he hides, then creeps out, like a creature in the woods after a storm—a storm that never happens, that he never goes through . . . a storm he avoids. Chris feels scathed by the disaster he evades. After a time in hiding, he gingerly reaches out again. He gets some nourishment by circling around potential bonds, tasting and retreating. He is left with himself as a disaster, rigidly modulating dreads searing impacts of originary bonds set in motion. The will to survive becomes a brittle hide-and-seek, unbearable fusions of dread and nourishment. It may be banal that many survive life by hiding from it, but terror mixed with nourishment has very real consequences.

"Lena"

Lena gripped therapy more tightly than Chris from the beginning. She came more often, she held on for dear life. Chris had difficulty letting therapy into his life, Lena could not live outside it. For years, therapy *was* Lena's life. To Chris, such need seemed like certain death. He could not bear seeing himself as "sick" as Lena felt.

Lena's mother was dying throughout her childhood. Her mother could never hold her fully and completely. Her mother's embrace was faulty. I do not think it only a matter of disease, although the latter was crucial. In photos that Lena showed me, her mother (attractive, well-intentioned, a good person) seemed not quite connected with the baby in a direct, immediate way. She loved and appreciated Lena, yet she seemed to look past or over her or to slide off her. It was as if she were already disappearing from her body, as the latter prepared to disintegrate. More, she seemed to be disappearing from her *self*, and perhaps this was happening long before illness gathered momentum.

I did not see the simple heart-to-heart connection mothers and babies have. Perhaps it was there in photos Lena did not show, or in memories Lena did not have. But I suspect the heart-to-heart connection, like mother's glance, tended to slide away. Glance rather than gaze? Lena's eyes tended to be glazed over, hazy, glassy, fixed in a pinpoint within themselves. What was outside seemed a distraction, and she had trouble concentrating, holding things together. She seemed to be focused on something invisible with no location at all. Something of searing intensity.

Perhaps she was her mother, trying to find her baby, trying to find the right way to see and hold a baby, a way to find and hold herself. Perhaps she was her mother's missing intensity. In Lena's memory, her mother seemed affable but always on the verge of fading away—fading away from herself as well as the baby and child: not only a fading-away mother, but a fading-away *person*— pleasant and well thought of, but not possessed of a full emotional register, not fully available to herself, let alone a baby. Yet she was good to people and good for people, if somewhat missing. Many individuals compensate in public for what is missing in intimacy (and *vice versa*).

Lena was intense with a vengeance. She was nothing if not intense. She was the spiritual fierceness lacking in her world. She felt like a sore thumb in her social milieu. She no more fitted in than did her mother's dying body. It would take many years before she discovered spiritual counterparts. She fought against fading away with fierce intensity—an intensity that, for a long time, had nowhere to go.

An anomaly of Lena's childhood with paralysing consequences was that no one acted as if her mother were dying. No one spoke of it. Even doctors acted as if she might get better, as body deteriorated and strength drained. When Lena tried to speak openly about her mother's illness, she was, in effect, shut up and made to feel guilty for not believing in recovery. An anti-truth-shield formed around her mother, a coating of lying doctors and aids. Lena could not even speak the truth with her father or with the woman hired to take care of her. There did not seem to be any truth in the family to speak. The fact that her mother became bedridden for years was a reality neither to be noticed nor disregarded.

In her own way, Lena was a loyal daughter. She grew up feeling she ought not to be noticed. She was in the predicament of bonding to a fading-away, deteriorating mother and fighting the bond. She was convinced she could not be seen. If she was seen, people would recoil. They would see her mother's death in her. She was the truth of her mother's death, the ugly truth, the unseen truth. She *was* the unacknowledged, witness to what must not be seen, outside everyone's system.

Her father loved her but was absorbed in himself—bigger than life in public, appreciated by his peers. With Lena, he was overwhelming or remote. When he beamed his warm emotionality towards her, she tended to cringe. His feelings took so much space, there seemed little room for her. She resented his love as well as his remoteness. She loved him, but she found his warmth self-serving. Love choked on hate. She felt bombarded then dropped, and inwardly she accused him for unfair outpourings of Eros and rage.

Her caretaker insidiously undermined what trust in self survived. She would insinuate that anyone interested in Lena really wanted something from her father. No one could want to be with her. Would the caretaker be with her if not for money? What favours must others want? Lena's aloneness felt boundless. Lena, too, was an only child, with no siblings to mitigate boundless aloneness.

Personalities mutate when pressured by such aloneness. Lena sought from God what she wanted in a mother. She sought from God a world she felt shut out of. Her spiritual talent became acute. But she also grew in inner cruelty. Her self-attacks were devastating. She tried to breathe through spirituality, but inner tightness suffocated her.

She felt stigmatized by spiritual interest. Her mystical bent meant that she was an outcast. Even her abilities were signs that she was off the map.

Yet something grew, a drill, a laser, sharp, deep, insistent. At the same time, there was cold, cruel contraction, barbed wire cutting in all directions, a critical eye turning body into a closed fist. Therapy elicited beginnings of a sense of compassion for her plight, permission to care for herself in face of mutilating internal indictments, support for moments of opening, softening.

Perhaps she drew on her father's warm expansiveness, although it frightened her. Perhaps a gentle background love from her mother seeped through. Perhaps she sometimes drilled through God's cruelty to tap a well of mercy. She used therapy to steer between lines of self, to touch the caring that came through the pain.

I could see the barbed wire close in and squeeze, self tightening into an unscreamed scream that would not let go. There seemed no end to hardening, the knot of a child refusing to cry, refusing adults the satisfaction of showing she could be hurt—mute, infinite injury, cushioned by a hope that therapy supported. Therapy emboldened Lena to draw on currents of love the inner spoiler furiously attacked. She ridiculed love for the ways it failed and exploited her. She stifled innate loving tendencies because they had nowhere to go.

It was not simply a matter of being unloved. It was more that no one knew what to do with love. What love there was, was subject to injury. Ambition, social life, vitality, egoism, disease, decrepitude ran over, neglected, exploited a child. The child was swept away, maimed, scattered by forces no one let themselves perceive. Lena became an expert at feeling pain. She could *see* the forces of injury. She made her painful case to the only being who might hear, the only One that might know, the only One that might do something, the Holy One, blessed be S/He. God, too, was in danger of crumbling but lasted long enough to find an opening. Lena's crumbling God swept her into therapy, not a moment too soon.

Often therapy has to begin when it almost seems too late. When Lena first sought me, she brought pain, scatter, disintegration, dread. Fury and grief were not far behind. Her God made a bad job of it and was no more to be trusted than anyone in life. As a matter of fact, if there was one thing she learned about God, it was that those who sought him were in for hell—and those who did not were in for hell too. She brought her pain to God, who seemed to make it worse.

We went into the God of hell together, with no thought of reaching heaven. In a bizarre way, I suspect, background intimations of the heavenly God make it somewhat possible to undergo such pain. Even in hell there is contact with heaven. We are bizarre creatures in a bizarre God—at times beautifully bizarre, but often a God of bizarre torments.

Lena was too far into God to get out. There was no out to get to. When one has gone so far, one must go farther. There may be no end to God, but there are different God zones. I know this is not so, according to traditional logic: God must be the same everywhere, equi-perfect. But when one jumps into the God of experience, one finds variably pulsating areas of joy and horror. One swims around, area to area, sudden cold/warm spots in a sea, dumbfounding brews of bliss and terror. Once one enters this God, there is nowhere else to go. One cannot get to another person without God as a link. If one is suspended in a ghastly God zone, access to others is horrifying.

The complementary truth—one has no access to God except through others—was less available to Lena when we began. Living the flow between God ↔ self ↔ others became possible only by going through horrible God-connections together, reconnecting and reconnecting, until God became less cruel.

Horror spreads through God and self alike. But sometimes there are better pockets of self, better pockets of God. A bit of God or self withstands hell for a time. Bits of good feeling unite, endure for a while. Such moments resonate, strengthen each other, so that God and self are not only horrible.

In Lena's case, swirls of good/bad feelings were welded to knots of will—bits of will broke off, hardened, shrunk; cold hard will fists, condensed temper fits, frozen pools of will going nowhere. For moments, there were larger will currents, mean will fused or oscillating with good will, sprays of warmer, kindlier moments when caring had a chance. It takes many years for personality to thaw.

Damaged bonds, damaged dream-work

Bion (1992, p. 59) writes of the possibility of dream-work breaking down—a breakdown in ability to process feelings. A person who can only say "I don't know" in lieu of saying "I feel this or that" may be suffering a breakdown in the capacity to note, sustain, and process affects. The very underpinning of emotional life, its background support, may be damaged.

One may be paralysed by anxiety. But one's capacity to process anxiety may be damaged. The sequence, feeling → image → word, for example, can be out of play or warped.

Bion (1992) links this breakdown in dream-work with "the need to prevent the synthesis, in the depressive position, of a frightening super-ego". It would take quite some space to explicate what Bion might have meant by this remark, so here I will only pick what I need for present concerns. My amplification or twists reflect my warp.

1. Fright. The personality has undergone a terrible fright, probably repeatedly, probably suddenly. It is likely that fright permeated the atmosphere the individual was born into or was a significant dimension or thread or grain in upbringing. The individual was born into a frightened and frightening world, a world in which being frightened plays a significant role.

2. Personality congealed or collapsed around or into the fright. In addition to permeating personality, fright is a kind of nucleus. It spreads through body, the way it feels to be a person, through character.

3. Once collapse happens, it is difficult to undo. There are usually areas of collapse, not "total" collapse. But when dream-work breaks down, we are speaking of something devastating. Of course, dream-work often breaks down. We break down— many ways—on a more or less temporary basis. Breakdown is part of daily and nightly life. Still, there is more chronic broken-down-ness or areas of breakdown, which never seem to heal, which simmer and seep in insidiously stifling ways.

4. In Bion's work, "frightful fiend" can be emotional truth. We are haunted by truths that are too frightening to think, endure, and work with. What if one discovers that one lives a lie or discovers the lie one lives? Truth can blow life out of the water. Truth explodes lives. We lack the capacity to meet truths about ourselves without destroying ourselves. We are living this edge of evolution now, learning to live frightened to death by opposite frights, dream-work nibbling at them.

5. Adrenal fright infinitizes and becomes an intractable Idea of Fright. A Platonic Idea of Fright dominates personality (à la Satan and demons, subsets of frights, small f's and big F). For example, a man whose father had never hit him, never physi-

cally abused him, is, nonetheless, terrified of men. His father's intermittent fury permanently stamped him with terror. More frightening than actual men and his actual father most of the time is the Idea of the Father. Terror floods the Idea of the Father, more frightening than the men in his life. Personality is stifled by this terror. Abrupt, alarming moments become an Eternal Idea, Eternal Reality, although the face on everyone's fright is different.

6. Once personality is set in the mould of terror, it is difficult to move on. It is frightening to move from paranoid-schizoid to depressive positions, from one fright to another. Between is frightening too. One is stuck in annihilation anxiety, yet growth activates even more dread. One is unable to risk annihilation one knows for annihilation one does not. Unknown dreads, associated with growth, approach on the horizon. They seem *too* dreadful. If the frightful truth be known, one has become attached or addicted to a state of collapse. One has grown used to the taste of oneself—the taste of one's own decay, the decay of one's psychic carcass.

7. In Bion's work, superego is not just Freud's paternal or Klein's maternal superego—it takes off from them. He points to an ominous hypertrophy of superego, superego parasiting on and devouring ego. Organ of morality becomes destroyer of self. Magnified superego severity contaminates, annexes, dissolves more and more of everything else. The *egodestructive superego* divorces "morality" from the quest for the Good and everyday ethics. Its morality is an empty, moralistic, tyrannical assertion of its own superiority and privilege (see Paul's, 1997, lacerating descriptions of superego's drive to devour and null personality and living).

    Selfdestructive superego is steeped in and draws power from generalized, formless dread—dread congealed into hate. Hate's enormous power draws on boundless dread. Hate plays the parasite on deeper energies. Rage is fed by terror.

8. Bion writes of the need to prevent synthesis of a frightening superego in the depressive position. On the one hand, there is hatred of reality. One is set against growth. One will not trade

superego superiority for mutuality. The force of dread has been funnelled through the frightening superego. Displacement of the latter's centrality has become impossible. Psychopathic cunning allied with megalomanic inflation energized by dread passing through rage has hardened into character.

The depressive position involves love/hate of a "whole" object with good/bad aspects. It implies incipient responsibility for damaging impulses, a sense that one can cause and repair damage. Repair works both ways. If one can repair the other, one can repair self. Caring and repairing, not only cruelty, are part of life. The annihilating superego is offset by capacity to repair.

Personality may be so absorbed by the annihilating superego that it is unable to tolerate the latter's synthesis into a larger whole (in which its hegemony is reduced). The need to preserve the *status quo*, to protect the fright one is used to, is identified with absorption by superego's posturing. One's own aims are silenced or fused with forces one is menaced by. A need to remain unborn becomes an imperative. The ability to process feelings through dream-work stays at a standstill. Dream after dream is reduced to signals of damage.

Selfdestructive superego as container of terror is a mock container.[2] The hate/dread pulsing through it obscures hardening of psychic arteries. In Lena's case, hardened pockets or balls of compressed will formed in opposition to superego tyranny. She could not be eaten and digested if she condensed enough. Self-tightening is survival. Will binds fright. To some extent, the strategy works but boomerangs. Tightening becomes tyrannical. Superego seeps into the tightening. One's personality becomes a noose—a barbed-wire noose. One is suffocated by oneself. Knots of will substitute for bonds that heal.

---

[2]If only it were as simple as making a distinction between True and False Self (Winnicott, 1960) or true and mock container! Often the two are indistinguishable, even reversible, varying in particular contexts. In real life, conceptual distinctions collapse, although they have uses. We try to let bits of strangulated states speak, expressing some ways people feel deformed, drawing attention to the sense of damage that seeks and hides from help.

In Chris's case, fantasy knots were bits of congealed will. Obsession with rape provided images for clots of will to nest in. Once will is embedded in fantasy, life becomes less compelling. A tendency for life to feed fantasy takes precedence over fantasy feeding life. In growth, they feed each other. Chris's life was caught in a fantasy skew that was a home for shards of will. Splinters of will, bound by rape fantasies, masked damaged/damaging bonds. Layers of fantasy wrapped damaged bonds, fantasy nests for shaky, unyielding scraps of will.

In Laura's case, damaged/damaging bonds worked their way out in relationships—and particularly in her marriage. For many years, her husband enacted the role of *selfdestructive superego*, reduced, empty, tyrannical will feeding on and reducing her life. A limit was placed on parasitism by oppositionalism. Each contracted to fight the other, with limits placed on devouring. They recoiled from each other enough to maintain a boundary. She contracted, too, to counter a tendency to dispersal (she tended to disperse, as her husband spread and annexed territory). Laura had a sixth sense that told her that she could heal, in spite of and with the aid of her marriage, with therapy help. She was able to use relationships to find resources in the face of damage.

* * *

What supports a dream supports a person. The ability to create a dream, to see an experience through, to process affects, to support a self—such generative work can suffer immense degradation. Damaged bonds damage unconscious processing. Unconscious processing tries, in part, to work with its damage. Such a circle can spiral—damage adding to damage. What damages a dream damages a person.

Therapy offers a potential bond to support the growth of unconscious processing. Unconscious processing is to the psyche what air or blood flow is to the body. Therapy affirms the reality of unconscious processing and helps to jump-start or reset the latter. We need a somewhat self-healing unconscious, but once the latter becomes self-damaging, we need another's unconscious to right things. Therapy provides a kind of auxiliary unconscious until one's own gets the hang of it.

Compassion in the background seeps into damage. It is not a case of saying or not saying. One feels the spot where hope dies out, where screams vanish and feelings disappear and rise again. One feels oneself coming back, a little less knotted, a bit more dependent on unconscious depths, will in water—another "feel", tone, guiding spirit, good angels in the air.

CHAPTER TWO

Wounded nourishment

M any of Bion's clinical examples contain the theme of wounded nourishment.

It is unclear whether: (1) there is a state of affairs one might call "primary nourishment", which gets wounded; (2) nourishment and woundedness are conjoined from the outset; (3) or nourishment and catastrophe have somewhat different tracks that are superimposed one on the other, or link up and permeate each other. These, as well as other possibilities, play some role in various passages.

At times one might say: "In the beginning there was nourishment."

At times one might say: "In the beginning there was catastrophe."

Bion's writings give voice to the traumatized self. If Walt Whitman sings the body electric and catalogues joys of self, Bion details what it is like for self to be electrocuted and to continue as the remains. If nourishment appears, something bad will happen to it.

Ice cream—I scream

In one vivid example, Bion (1970, pp. 13–14) traces a nourishing link through successive phases of destruction. He is more interested in what becomes of the scream as link than the fate of food as link. But he points to a primary nourishing link undergoing waves of disturbances resulting in waves of destruction.

If one creates a temporal narrative of Bion's description, one might say: "In the beginning was the good breast—a nourishing situation or potentially nourishing situation." Life as sea of nourishment, the cornucopia aspect of life, plenitude. Before screaming, nourishment links personalities.

> The "'I scream" link had itself previously been food, "ice-cream", a "breast", until envy and destructiveness had turned the good breast into an "I scream". In narrative form: he had been linked to his object by a good breast (he liked ice-cream). This he had attacked, possibly bitten in actuality. The place of the breast as link was then taken by an "I scream". [Bion, 1970, p. 13]

Biting the apple. William Blake depicts the garden—all is well, then evil shows up. The serpent in the garden, part of Adam and Eve's disposition: disturbance, restlessness, envy. Punch and Judy meet the devil.

The scream replaces the breast as link between personalities. A taste of heaven, the beginning of hell.

The good object is linked with nourishment, physical and mental. Destruction turns up and screaming substitutes for satisfaction. Bion is most keenly Bion in depicting destructive transformations of the scream as link. He is particularly master of the fading scream, the scream that dies forever, background radiation of spaceless space, the dispersed scream (Eigen, 1996, 1998, 1999).

An attacking process gathers momentum, moves past the scream itself, silences screaming. The "I scream" becomes a "no—I scream": growth of negativism towards stupor, ever-increasing self-obliteration. The psyche freezes, falls silent, drops out of existence. From "No, I won't even scream" to "I can't scream", as one is stricken with horror, especially horror of one's own destructiveness and destruction.

A further result is destruction of the link itself. Bion visualizes this as an explosion of the linking process as such—fragments of link instantaneously dispersed through infinite mental space. Silence explodes. The "transference" in analysis is, partly, this explosion stretched into "an extremely thin membrane of a moment":

> the total analysis can be seen as a transformation in which an intense catastrophic emotional explosion O has occurred (elements of personality, link, and second personality having been instantaneously expelled to vast distances from their point of origin and from each other). [Bion, 1970, p. 14]

From nourishment to explosive wipe-out.

Mug of beer

In the Introduction to *Attention and Interpretation*, Bion again gives an example in which nourishment and violence are conjoined:

> The patient says, "Suddenly, just as I finished lunch he threw a mug of beer in my face without any warning. I kept my head and showed no resentment at all remembering what you said about psycho-analysis. So it passed off without anyone noticing." [Bion, 1970, p. 3]

Bion asks whether the patient is lying? Hallucinating? What does one make of such a communication? Does one have instruments to evaluate it? (See also Eigen, 1999, pp. 144–148.)

He gives this example in a discussion of the "all-pervading nature" of lying in the human race. Unlike many investigators, who feel that a liar cannot be psychoanalysed, Bion raises the spectre of a deeper difficulty. To put it dramatically: if a liar cannot be psychoanalysed, who can? (See also Bollas, 1987, ch. 10; O'Shaughnessy, 1990.) Part of the social reaction against psychoanalysis is rooted not simply in fear of self-discovery, but in fear of psychoanalytic lying, all the more dangerous when disguised as truth-seeking.

The vision Bion provides goes further. Legalistic and rationalistic distinctions between lying and truth miss deeper problems involving areas in which truth and lying can be indistinguishable. Language itself evolved as an instrument of deception and conceal-ment as much as to convey truth. What does it mean when one person accuses another of lying? The situation is often such that the accuser has his or her own devious, nasty scenario embedded in a sense of injury or self-righteousness. It is no accident that the devil is an accuser, a prosecutor, searching out evil in others to match his own—the father of lies, a truth monger.

The issue is all the more pressing in light of Bion's association of truth as food for the mind, lying as poison. The situation we live is often characterized by toxic nourishment (Eigen, 1999)—not only nourishment with toxic elements or toxins with nourishing compo-nents, but the more vertiginous discovery of poison and nourish-ment mixed beyond discernment.

For example, the patient's communication above. On the one hand, it is a caricature of psychoanalysis. The analyst keeps his head in emotionally charged situations. The patient exaggerates and rigidifies the analyst's invitation to observe and explore expe-rience, in fact nullifies it. An emotionally charged situation is met with no emotion, shutting off, not noticing.

The movement from nourishment to nullity parallels the fall from nourishment into scream/no-scream/explosive nothingness. As so often in Bion's sketches, the change is abrupt, alarming, sudden: "suddenly", "without any warning". Just as the person finishes a decent feed, violence erupts. He cannot enjoy the full arc of a good experience, including the aftermath. The good arc is interrupted, displaced by turbulence, emotional flooding, shock. The shock of recognition: oh–oh, the bad thing is happening again. Traumatized nourishment is followed by an attempt to regain sta-bility. The end result is a dampening of emotionality. The person attempts to achieve minimal or no emotion in the face of a rising emotional storm. As emotional flooding rises towards a maximum, emotional shutting-off increases. A position of maximum/mini-mum emotion is achieved. The very expression of self in talking to an analyst points to violent self-nullification.

The issue of whether or not the patient is lying or hallucinating gives way to reading the fate of emotional reality. Whether the patient ate lunch and was attacked or provoked the attack and turned the other cheek—whatever meanings or avoidance of meaning can be assigned to such imaginary/real events—the fate of the emotional being of a person rings loud and clear. The conjunction of nourishment, violence (e.g. attacks on nourishment) and shutting down (refusal or inability to feel) comes through as real, whatever the gloss. Emotional violence, violation of emotional life, traumatized nourishment is central, although we may not be sure what to make of it. Whatever the issues of the war, the wounds are real.

Cut off

In a 1959 entry to his "intellectual diary", *Cogitations* (1992, p. 29), Bion relates a patient's abrupt use of language to cut off exploration of awareness that a primary object "cut off supplies". The patient is talking about not having enough money for *food* if he sells stock shares to pay for a vacation, then cuts off discussion by saying, "That's all there is to it." When Bion calls attention to this breaking off, the patient over-blames himself and veers away from experiencing "the existence of a very bad obstructive object".

Again we have a situation of traumatized nourishment. Bion's psychoanalytic vision pulls together the patient's cut-off use of language, cut-off feelings, and substitution of fruitless self-blame for perception of "a very bad obstructive object". Self-blame here is a kind of self-affirmation, a self-protective narcissistic/autistic shield to escape a realization of devastating damage outside one's control.

One might wonder whether the damaging object is the phantasy of mother damaged by the patient's aggression, or whether a destructive mother created situations in which provision of nourishment was overly wounding, or both. Whatever the cause, the result is an individual's difficulty in extending himself to cover a wider range of experiencing. The individual is used to cutting off when feelings build. In the current example, feelings = dangerous object.

The analyst becomes a dangerous object if he invites exploration of feelings. If analysis suggests that the patient's mother is "a very dangerous object denying him food", a pillar of the patient's psychic life is threatened. Bion's psychoanalytic vision gravitates towards a sense of damaged/damaging foundations one is too terrified to experience. In the current instance, nourishment becomes a signifier of danger. Nourishment means that something bad is about to happen—the sense of the goodness/fullness of life will get cut off. A nourishing object is a dangerous object; nourishment and destruction are fused.

In such a situation rise of feeling that might nourish personality is felt as dangerous, permeated by an apprehension of something bad happening. Feeling, fused with a sense of impending disaster, itself comes to be a danger. A devastating consequence is that the advent of emotion becomes a signal to shut off emotion. Disaster or dread of disaster is "solved" by having no feeling, substituting one disaster for another. In this predicament, feeling and no feeling signify disaster—from pan to fire or firelessness (see also Eigen, 1996, Ch. 16, "Disaster Anxiety"). The patient, terrified by the possibility that any feeling might be annihilating, cuts himself off each time he tries to communicate the danger he feels. The analyst, spokesperson for feeling, may seem an ally of danger, asking the patient to stay in harm's way.

Feelings nourish us. If we must cut off feelings to cut off danger, we become emotional anorexics. If we begin starving ourselves of feeling, it is a small step to become emotional gorgers and purgers. With little effort, Bion's descriptions easily become a contemporary morality play: can nourishment survive what we do to it? It is, too, no accident that Bion is fascinated with the symbolic link of money and food. Can emotional nourishment survive our manic addiction to money?

The entry in *Cogitations* where the above quote appears is entitled, parenthetically, "4:30 a.m. Blast it!" Yes, Bion is annoyed that he is up 4:30 a.m., with his patient's words and state going round in his mind. Apparently he cannot successfully cut off from his patient, not enough to sleep through the night. His patient's cut-off state cuts into him, keeps him up, exercises him. He uses his patient's cut-off state as a tool for reflection.

The coupling of violence and nourishment cuts through many levels. The innocent-sounding "Blast it!" has ghastly resonances in Bion's work. I recall his repeated descriptions of soldiers next to him suddenly being blown open, organs exposed, and the grisly, uncanny reality of a body dying before the consciousness it was supposed to support. Bion said he suffered the reverse fate, since he died, in some way, as a personal being while his body remained alive. All this doubtless fed his preoccupation with a state of affairs too ghastly to experience, emotional shock and shut-down, endowment not up to what it must go through. Nourishment as prelude to disaster, or, more in keeping with the spirit of a core Bion preoccupation, nourishment and disaster as indistinguishable. This involves both a sense of normalcy being suddenly and violently ruptured and a sense that rupture is normal.

Object-seeking

In an undated entry in *Cogitations* (1992, pp. 34–35), Bion associates the activity of *seeking* with three "tropisms". One seeks "(1) an object to murder or be murdered by, (2) a parasite or host, (3) an object to create or by which to be created." All three are summed for the patient who comes for treatment as "a seeking for an object with which projective identification is possible".

Too many analysts, I fear, make patients feel guilty for parasitic–murderous tendencies and find difficulty tolerating areas of creation as well. These three forms of object-seeking are fused, but Bion affirms that if a patient seeks an object for projective identification, the area of creation is dominant (no matter how obscured or threatened by countertendencies).

Bion links the importance of projective identification in treatment to developmental failure. When inevitable trauma occurs, "all the future development of the personality depends on whether an object, the breast, exists into which tropisms can be projected. If it does not, the result is disaster which ultimately takes the form of loss of contact with reality, apathy, or mania."

Personality is object-seeking or has object-seeking needs, drives, requirements (here named "tropisms"). Parasitic, murderous, creative needs require another being, a partner, for processing, sharing, for contact with reality. We reach for reality in many ways, with amazing fusions of creative/destructive tendencies. It is all too easy for reality to fail us, all too easy to have urges with no place to go.

For Freud it was common sense that mothering aims at alleviating baby's distress. Ferenczi depicts the mother taking the edge off the death drive and reconciling the baby to life. Bion picks up this thread and amplifies Klein's notion of projective identification as a medium for building the sense of contact. Successful projective identification sustains the sense that human contact is necessary and possible. It supports hope.

So often psychoanalysis emphasizes frustration and break of object contact as crucial for building a sense of reality and capacity for symbol formation. It is important to balance this with emphasis on the actual presence and work of the object in supporting an infant's sense of reality. A parent may be hard pressed and bewildered by infantile distress, but without a worthy try, the spectre of falling into unreality gains power.

The basic situation is fraught with difficulties. Bion depicts an infant's seeking tendencies as too strong for its own personality—and perhaps too much for parents as well. The possibility that as a species we may be too much for ourselves is a theme that runs through Bion's work. Our task is an evolutionary challenge. Can we take ourselves? Can we take what we put into each other? Bion suggests that we cannot take ourselves unless we can take each other. At the same time, capacity to take one another is poorly evolved. We do not take each other very well. We hope that the ability to do so grows and that the capacity to support mutuality presses further into existence because of need and practice.

A personality may have supported and collapsed areas, less and more psychotic aspects. In his "tropism" account, Bion links the development of psychotic parts of personality to the breast's intolerance of projective identification. Tropism is part of the projecting, object-seeking personality. An object responding to murderous/parasitic/creative urges with overabundance of anxiety, persecution, hate, apathy throws the self back on unmodified aggravated urges.

The search for help meets an intolerant object that becomes a model for "self-help" (i.e. intolerance of self, self-murder). The need to communicate reaches an anxious, hostile environment and

learns that communication is impossible or dangerous. One's attitude towards communication becomes negative, cynical, or worse
(in the "ice cream/I scream/no-I scream example, communication
as linking function is depicted as explosively shattering into lost,
wayward, meaningless, and dangerous particles).

Nourishment in the current context is the object's ability to
modify the mess of murder/parasitism/creativeness so that personality can use its tendencies decently. Breakdown of this modify-
ing capacity results in a breakdown of the communicating capacity
and a loss of contact with reality. Contact with reality is dependent
on work others do for us when we reach out. To be nourishing
means helping personality survive its projections, enabling projection to be a tool of communication and self-control, fostering matri-
ces in which we use each other to grow.

The unseeable/unspeakable object

A result of object-seeking meeting an intolerant object (intolerant of
projective identification) is dread of dreaming or the incapacity to
dream or relate to dreams. After describing semi-collapse and
shutting off of self in face of an object's incapacity to feel or let
baby's feelings in or work with feelings well, Bion's diary entries
for over 60 pages (Bion, 1992, pp. 37–98) are concerned with the
destruction of the capacity to dream. The capacity to dream is
allied with the capacity to feel and process feelings.

Bion's writings on the destruction of the capacity to dream and
feel are quite complex, and I must be very selective in what I
highlight here. The capacity to be nourished by life (and to nourish
life) are wounded at the root, if one is too terrified to dream what
must be dreamt, if one dare not dream the object that stops dreaming.

What must be dreamt are the very destructive processes that
destroy dreaming. How is this possible? The whole point of analysis, in this situation, is to create a situation that supports growth of
capacity to dream the necessary dream. The analyst, with whatever
flaws and failings, is a signifier that psychic life is possible and
necessary, and that the state of affairs that cannot be dreamt (or

felt, expressed, discussed, worked with) must be, and sooner or later can be, at least in part.

The object that cannot be dreamt can be partly described as a "murderous superego" (Bion, 1992, p. 37), made up of the object's failure to support projective identification, the collapse of object-seeking tendencies, magnification of the horror of not being able to reach another's insides with one's own, reaching only traumatizing outsides. Bion is at his blood-curdling best describing disintegration products of personality, such as tropisms breaking up into malignant debris, the very failure of the quest for nourishment turning into radioactive self-poisoning states, results of breakdown endlessly breaking down, so that proliferating diffusion becomes rigidified.

In such a ghastly scenario, personality comes under dominance, more or less, by an anti-feeling, anti-dreaming, anti-psyche tendency, which includes the intolerant object magnified and further distorted by traumatized/traumatizing emotional intensity. Personality becomes intolerant of itself. Emotional processing is jammed. Rise of emotion becomes a signal to shut down. Bits of hallucination, frozen and strangulated feeling, menacing or barren thoughts coagulate into impacted residues of shock.

In a sense, the patient *is* what he needs to *dream*. The patient needs help in dreaming himself. He needs to begin processing terror, breakdown, and paralysed states by dreaming about his inability to process breakdown, not simply being it. The patient comes for help to dream the undreamable, for help in activating and tolerating dream-work.

The patient is terrified to assemble a dream in which the dreaded object or object beyond dread may appear. There are references in myths and stories about dying if too bad or good an object is seen or touched (Medusa, God). In such instances, too much dread or terror or awe surrounds ineffable beauty and the grotesque. Yet it is precisely depths of death and shards of madness and the mad/maddening object that dream-work must endure or, at least, express. If one is trapped outside life (outside dreaming) or in anti-life (anti-dream), one begins the journey towards communication by at first encoding bits of death and breakdown in dreams, like messages in a bottle. One can only dare this if desperation meets support.

He [the patient] therefore postpones this experience till the analytic session in which he hopes he will have the support, or perhaps, feeling he has the support, dares to have the dream he cannot have without the consciousness of support. [Bion, 1992, p. 37]

To dream one's madness or deadness means that a modicum of creation prevails in the midst of parasitism and murder. Even a minimally successful dream is a tribute to human contact, an act of faith.

Some minimal complexities

Bion is mainly concerned not with what dreams conceal but with what they reveal ("He [Freud] took up only the negative attitude, dreams as 'concealing' something, not the way in which the *necessary* dream is *constructed*"(Bion, 1992, p. 33). Bion is especially concerned with traumatized depths, mangled personality, and the struggle to communicate ghastly states in dreams. Dreaming is a place to try to piece oneself together; it reflects attempts at emotional processing. In dreams we tear ourselves and our objects apart, rearrange ourselves, piece ourselves and our objects together in variable ways.

To reiterate, Bion believes that a primary block to dreaming is dread of assembling an object too terrifying to dream, an object that explodes dreaming. One cannot dream (or must cut off relationship to dreaming) because the object supporting dreams fails to appear or fails to make an effective enough appearance. Instead, one is in the position of trying to dream an anti-dream object, an object inimical to processing emotional life. The analysis, bad as it is, provides a counter-pole, a support for emotional life, a support for dreaming. Little by little, the anti-dream Medusa/God is spotted, dream life builds courage.

The object that cannot be dreamt, the anti-dream object, is often an amalgam of damaged/damaging primary objects (actions and aspects of mother/father/caretakers/milieu) fused with mutilated parts of personality, which agglutinate/disperse/compress and undergo deformed magnification and rigidification.

Bion refers to innate beauty as well: beatific objects, objects of light, light itself. For example, he associates luminosity with changes of pressure in the optic pits while in the womb (1991, p. 486). Luminosity has physiological aspects but also plays a vital role in spiritual and psychological dimensions. "Horny-handed tons of soil soil the white radiants of eternity and turn them into many-coloured life" (1991, p. 51). He speaks of the stainless light and the stain of life. Thus the meaning of wounded nourishment undergoes twists and turns. The light is nourishing, indeed. But so is the stain of life. Both intertwine in nourishing, devastating ways. One may cling to the Light in the face of daily injuries or cling to everyday wounds and triumphs and mock the Light (see, e.g., at times, Lena). But it is also possible to open oneself, to whatever extent one can, to the play of dimensions that constitute experience and ways they spontaneously arrange themselves. To some extent—we do not know to what extent—such a capacity develops by using it.

As if to underline the magnitude of the challenge, Bion calls the "helpless infant" a "growing annihilating force" (1991, p. 61). The impact of new life—actual and potential—can be too much to bear. The parents shut the infant out or deform it in order to avoid being annihilated. In this context, the infant's impact is the Medusa/God that cannot be sustained. The infant puts too much into the other's insides—too much aliveness, deadness, sameness, otherness, raw intensity, urge to grow without knowing how to. The infant threatens to awaken the parent to an aliveness that pushes life out of cages, at the same time chaining parents to its needs. One does what one can to shrink the infant into what is workable. At the same time, Bion fears that if the infant were not too much, it would not be noticed.

We have a cast of annihilating objects or subjects, including infant and parents, pure luminosity of eternity and the colourful stains of life, destructiveness of growth or inability to perceive and support the latter. To an extent, we are all burnt-out versions of ourselves, watered-down ways of handling destructive forces, residues of emotional intensity. The dread we dread is not only the ghastly object that throws us back on ourselves in maddening ways (intolerant object ↔ terrifying superego), but dread of annihilating emotional intensity as such.

It seems clear that the attempt is inherent to ward off, or to ward off awareness of something which is dread or terror and behind that the object that is nameless. [Bion, 1991, p. 77]

Pain (or ecstasy) accruing to creative growth or damage may be part of nameless dread objects, good or bad. At times the pain can be so impalpable and intense and pure (Bion, 1991, pp. 51–52) that personality tries to destroy it, even if it means destroying the physical form that appears to support it. At such a moment one may try both to escape and to find the nameless object in a permanent dreamless state.

Glimpses of destruction:
nourishment comes through

One of Bion's most vivid portrayals of a feelingless state, in which even dreams are empty, is the following:

The dreamless sleep ended. The day was as empty of events—facts proper to daytime—as the night had been empty of dreams. Meals were served to both girls. It occurred to them that they had no memory of the food; the "facts" of daytime and night were defective, mutilated. They were having dreams—mutilated dreams—lacking a dimension like a solid body that casts no shadow in light. Thoughts with and thoughts without a thinker replaced a universe where discrimination ruled. Dreams had none of the distinguishing characteristics of mind, feelings, mental representations, formulations. The thinker had no thoughts, the thoughts were without thinkers. Freudian dreams had no Freudian free associations. Freudian free associations had no dreams. Without intuition they were empty; without concept they were blind. [Bion, 1991, p. 33]

He is describing a semi-annihilated, denuded psyche, a psycheless psyche, a psyche bereft of psychic life. One's relationship to nourishment is mutilated, defective. Dreams, feelings, thoughts—the food of mental life—do not nourish. Internal/external facts do not nourish. Connections fall away. Perhaps even the sense of mutilation disappears.

Yet life ticks on. Life reconstitutes itself through the flotsam and jetsam. Bits of life flicker, press for renewal, for resurgence. There are some 550 pages more to come after the above passage in *A Memoir of the Future*, which express and portray aspects of a struggling, gasping psyche to develop a signature and leave an imprint. Traumatic impacts of life are detailed, including extreme difficulties that feeling beings face, pressures that threaten to blow the capacity to think and to feel away. The book strips everything away, provides little consolation, but itself is nourishing—a wounded kind of nourishment. Creative work deals with pressures against creativity.

An underlying faith meets the hard facts of life, including collapse or destruction of the capacity to feel. There is a faith in Bion's work that something gets through, without minimizing difficulties. If anything, Bion maximizes difficulties to make sure that they are grappled with, or, at least, noted. He points to facts of destructiveness (human, inhuman, non-human) and says: "Look, this is there." Our psyche cannot handle its own aliveness—nor can we handle each other's aliveness. But intermittently we try. We throw ourselves into life and make the best of it. We think and feel as much as we dare or are able, as much as our bent equipment, desire, luck, ability, circumstances permit and then some. We shrink in the face of immensity, but we thrive on it too.

Wounds filter nourishment. Nourishment itself has toxic aspects. Bion uses the term "mutilated" a great deal. It is a perennial challenge and ordeal of feeling, thinking beings that intermixtures of nourishment and mutilation take living to new places.

CHAPTER THREE

Damaged dream-work

Dreams try to represent what hurts and weave a wombing effect around it, but the womb keeps breaking apart. Dreams as wombs attempt to contain and limit pain and generate new possibilities, but they often are damaged, even blown away, by trauma they try to display, undo, or work with. We try both to evade and to face our reality, our traumas, and to magnify, minimize, celebrate them, not simply to master them or be in bondage to them, but also to free ourselves from them. Dreams try to open freeing paths, but much of dream-work is crippled.

Dreams both contain and free. As womb for wounds, dreams not only represent the latter but infiltrate, permeate, and play a role in digesting injury. The womb image implies, too, transformation and birth—perennial beginnings. As a cocoon for wounds, dreams provide an arena for transformative work in the depths of wounds. But there are different kinds of containers, some more rigid, dead, airtight. There are containers for sealing psychic radioactive waste as long as possible and containers with permeable membranes for creative passage and commingling of material.

A fossil involves a containing process, and a fossilized dream may contain an image or imprint of life that is no longer. Some bit of psychic structure, process, possibility is embedded in a dream with nowhere to go but further decay if a dream does not preserve it. In this sense, dreams are a kind of embalming fluid, storing images of life that might have been. On the other hand, a dream that contains radioactive waste may do more than arrest decay. Corrosion and seepage lead to further destruction, at times global and random. Dreams and processes that create them can be part of destructive waves that go on and on.

The term "fossilized dream" implies a dream that not only acts as a fossil container but is a fossil itself. For example, a dream stuck within a dream may be fossilized dream-work. In certain instances, dreams strung out in a night or dream period can be fossils/containers of each other—parts of larger fossilizing process. In this case the dream is not a live container but part of a system in collapse. Part of what is collapsing is dream-work itself.

Bion (1992, p. 67) distinguishes between true dream and dream as artefact. The former is felt as life-promoting. It aids the digestion of psychic material, plays a role in linking feelings with images with ideas, and is part of a flow of psychic and intersubjective possibilities. Bion feels that such dreams or use of dreams are rare. Usually, dreams are signs of psychic indigestion, part of a universal deficiency or inability to digest emotional experience. They portray and are part of breakdowns in dream-work. *In extremis*, they evacuate the possibility of dream-work.

What ordinarily passes for dreams are dreams *manqué*, dreams masquerading as dreams, dream substitutes, bits of psychic indigestion, semi-breakdown, or disability. At one level, this can mean simply that dreams fail to be part of the web of dreaming. This is akin to a thought failing to be part of a network of thinking or a feeling failing to be part of a nexus of feelings. That is to say, it is possible for a thought to appear without finding a thinking process to engage it. For a thought to be meaningful, it has to be worked with, masticated, turned about, drawn out, linked with other thoughts. One follows or discovers associative networks or threads or leaps, as if riding magic carpets to new territory.

For a dream to be dreamt, it must find a dreamer (see Grotstein, 1983, 2000), enter into a dreaming process, engage the dreamer's life or cosmos, reverberate through many soul chambers, bear fruit in reflective imagination. It must be lived and responded to. It must be felt to be something living, something to care about. If it is a dead dream, it must, at least, be felt to be about something that has once lived, or might have lived, or lives in hiding still, or, grief be true, a confession of deadness or a prayer of death.

I am not emphasizing active engagement of the dream or active intentionality. A dream is probably dead or alive long before it reaches a point of consciousness where we can engage it. The soil from which it grows is more alive or dead, fertile or languishing before factors having to do with active/passive, conscious/unconscious mean much. Is the psychic subsoil rich enough to support life? Do surrounding conditions nourish it? Conscious intentions play a role in such questions, but depths of being matter more.

Alive dreams try to process bits of emotional experience. They are links in long chains of tries. They may gnaw at impasse points over the course of decades, even lifetimes. I suspect some "common" dreams shared by the species are, partly, attempts to work with common problems and obstacles. It may take centuries, even millennia, of dreaming certain dreams to begin working with obdurate difficulties.

Dreaming makes things real. Perhaps I should say that dreaming makes things *feel* real. This is an odd claim to make for something people dismiss as "It is only a dream. After all, it isn't real." How can something that is not real make things feel real? If for Freud dreams are the royal road to the unconscious, for Bion they are a road to the real. What kind of unconscious? What kind of real? How are they linked? Does something have to be unconscious in order to be real? Does it have to be unconscious in an alive way in order for what is real to feel real?

Bion coined the term "dream-work–alpha" to suggest a psychic activity that transforms raw external/internal impacts into material suitable for storage and recall. It is akin to Freud's primary process, but rather than feeding discharge, it aims at readying experience for attention and interest. Thus Bion teases out of Freud's writings a sense in which primary process does work. It plays a role in initiating a kind of binding and notation of impacts, so that the latter can begin to be worked on—symbolized, narrated, imaged, and the like.

In a number of passages, Bion (1992, pp. 51–52, 56, 59, 64, 71) describes the importance of pictures or ideograms in dream-work–alpha. Dream-work–alpha forms ideograms out of impacts so that aspects of the latter can be stored, recalled, reworked. Sets of feelings can be compressed into ideograms that serve as notations interacting with other notations, drawing attention, interest, and elaborative activity.[1] Bion feels that there is precision to these concretizations, nodes, or summary points of experience that can be unpacked over time.

Bion does not polarize "concrete" and "abstract" in these passages. On the contrary, if there is a contrast, it is between alpha working (whether concretely or abstractly) or not working. He feels that dream-work–alpha is involved with making mathematics as well as elemental coding of feelings. If alpha is alive and well, there is good flow between concretization ↔ abstraction and infinite gradations between them (and they are always fused). An amazing tap dancer has good alpha function living in his feet, a great piano player has alpha hands (probably good heart–brain–gut–hand connections), a mystical visionary who extends our sense of life has "alpha vision". The point is not to get from concrete to abstract but to get to alpha.

Bion uses the terms "dream-work", alpha, "dream-work–alpha" in similar and overlapping if not always completely interchangeable ways. The overall point he makes is the same. Waking life is dependent on dream life. Dreams store raw impacts and play a role in the work that makes them communicable. Dream-work is continuous; it goes on while we are asleep or awake. Impressions from outside/inside are transformed by dream-work and made available for further work by consciousness, selection, attention, memory, unconsciousness, repression, and all manner of revisions, amplifications, extensions. Dream-work plays a role in creative activity and digestion of experience from bottom up (or almost bottom up).

In passing, I wish to note the importance of the image (conscious and/or unconscious) in Bion's thinking. In line with an aspect of romantic epistemology, the image is not a second-class

---

[1] Graham Sleight (personal communication) links such ideograms with mandalic activity described by Jung.

citizen but plays a basic role in readying experience for mental digestion and feeds the digestive process in many ways. Images are primal filters or way-stations for experiential impacts and act as conduits for sorting emotional valences and elemental gripping moments. They are a kind of "language" conveying emotional nuances, the "feel" of things, directional pressures, even a sense of truth and falsehood. There is much imageless processing too, and sometimes processing seems to move through "muscular feels". It may be that dream-work begins below or outside the image and transmutes raw feels through image filters on the way towards discovery and action. What comes through Bion's writings on dreams is his acute valuing of alpha, however fragmented, mute, awkward, faltering, whatever level or form. It is not a matter of image versus idea, but whether image/idea is part of alpha functioning, remains outside it, or substitutes for it.

Dream-work–alpha helps to metabolize conscious and unconscious "material". It masticates, dissolves, reconnects inputs from diverse fields of being, pre-verbal and verbal. Bion hints that dream-work helps consciousness seep into deep regions of being, so that it becomes available for unconscious processing. Dream-work has a linking function, enabling reciprocal flow between depth/surface and conscious/unconscious life.

It is not a matter, as for Freud, of decoding the unconscious into conscious terms. Unconscious work is not consciousness in disguise. Consciousness itself has to be subjected to a process that runs through consciousness/unconsciousness. What is outside alpha—conscious or unconscious, verbal or preverbal—has to undergo dream-work–alpha in order to enter the stream of psychic nourishment.

Dream-work–alpha and its linking function is damaged or destroyed in actual "psychosis". One reason people say the psychotic has no unconscious—that it all pours out—has to do with damage to dream-work–alpha. Some psychotics are too conscious of the unconscious, or not unconscious enough, or unconscious (or rejecting) of important aspects of consciousness. Here alpha function fails to transform aspects of consciousness into usable parts of unconscious work. Significant portions of conscious life are felt to be unreal because dream-work fails to transmute/digest them. Consciousness cannot work well because dream-work is injured.

Consciousness needs a good working unconscious to support it or undergoes warp and semi-collapse. Of central concern is whether alpha is enabling good conscious ↔ unconscious flow or whether something is wrong with alpha.

What does alpha work on? What can we say of outside/inside impacts that get transmuted by dream-work–alpha? Kant's things-in-themselves? Noumena? Plato's Ideas? Bion's O? Beta elements? If we say anything about "them", have they not already been transformed?

Bion (1992, pp. 63–65) tries to imagine what experience untransformed by alpha might be like by depicting it as being bereft of associations. He gives examples of a sensation or emotional experience devoid of a frame of reference. A table may loom in the visual field as a thing that appears, without any sense of what that thing is or how it functions. To call it a thing is a loose way of speaking as it may not even have the sense of thing. The same can be said of "experiences that appear to be those of emotion, fear, anxiety, dread, to which the patient seems unable to attach either a name or an image, or to recognize them as corresponding to any verbal expression he has ever heard or uttered."

It may be impossible to get to an experience that alpha has not worked on. Bion, in the tradition of philosophical/psychological reduction, pares experience down to what is most raw, stripping meaning away. Titchener, for example, did this by artificially creating conditions where bits of colour or sound were abstracted from context. Kant imagined chaotic sensations requiring transcendental organization, deep structures of mind moulding sensory flow. Freud's narcissistic ego "unified" chaotic auto-erotic streaming. Merleau-Ponty pictured form decomposing when focusing on the raw texture of stone that makes up the wall of a building (building fades, wall fades, self dissolves in texture, world vanishes in grains). What would the world be like, asks Condorcet, for a man (or consciousness or body) with all senses, four senses . . . three senses . . . two senses . . . one sense? No sense?

To get to pure sensation, one has to abstract from the flow of living experience—perform a reduction. This takes imagination. One can perform different sorts of reductions, depending on what one wants to abstract and what one wants to get at. Husserl, for example, abstracted three "I's" from the flow of experience: empirical I, psychological I, transcendental I. Husserlians felt that more than three would be redundant. Sartre felt that three was one too many. (It was enough to speak of self-transcending consciousness, i.e. consciousness aware of itself and not aware of being aware of being aware of itself.)

Gestalt psychologists tried to show that experience is already organized at the level of sensation. Form and structure is part of perception and sensation. One need not posit higher levels of organization to create order in lower ones. Experience is ordered from the ground up—spontaneously, inherently. Organizational processes shape the distribution of planetary bodies, distribute nourishment through blood flow, and give us our perceptual world. It is artificial to imagine events without frames of reference if everything is composed of processes reshaping themselves. Two points in a blank field refer to one another. Is there a single point alone?

Bion's depiction of experience prior to alpha work is something like a single point alone. An emotion appears—but will it become part of the tapestry of feelings? A thought appears—but will someone think it? A sensation appears—without a world to embrace it. Can one imagine an object lacking all associations? In trying to convey what he means by "table" without references, Bion writes: "It is as if the word is a counterpart of the pure note in music, devoid of undertones or overtones; as if, meaning nothing but 'table', it came near to meaning nothing at all" (Bion, 1992, p. 63).

And what would an emotion without references be like? An example Bion gives (p. 65) is a powerful emotional experience in a dream with no other content, an impinging emotion without a context. The fact that everything has a context makes a no-context emotion impossible to grasp. A no-context emotion stops emotional flow or is outside emotional flow or appears in gaps of emotional meaning. Alpha activity tries to create a possible world out of impossible emotions.

An emotion without a context can be of positive or negative valence, dreadful or ecstatic or both. It can be explosive or silent. It may seem to come from nowhere or be nowhere itself. People report a wide range of possibilities. Here is a patient's account with a positive cast: "I stumbled upon the place emotions come from, like a spot water bubbles up from to become a spring. Raw feelings are produced there. Joy, rage, fear, pain, sorrow—the spectrum. They keep coming, not attached to anything. They don't mean anything but just are. It's like going to the movies and seeing colour after colour without people or action attached to them. Strange at first, but I can get into it and be with it and go on like that."

Sometimes it is blankly eerie. "I stared at the feeling staring at me. It had the eye of a marlin that looks the same whether it is dead or alive. Did you ever see the eye of a dead marlin off the boat? It stares blankly. It is blankness itself. If you see it swimming in the water it has the same blank stare. That's what emotions are—blank eyes of a fish. They are what they are in death or life."

Is it up to alpha to warm things up? to give testimony to the chill? to say it like it is or imaginatively elaborate?

There is an urge to rip things apart, tear them until you reach an untearable place, shred experience until it becomes unshreddable. Find rock-bottom end points. You cannot rest until you find the basic elements, the building blocks, until you can find no more by destruction. But where a view arises that claims that sensations are basic building blocks, another says sensations cannot account for impalpable awareness or intuition. Right brain/left brain, old brain/new brain, doubleness/mystery.

Where before we meditated on pure sensation, now we can meditate on pure emotion. An emotion with no overtones or under-tones. With no undertow. And we posit or intuit infra-/ultra-range emotions with no face or shape at all or with, perhaps, expressions as yet unknown—emotions glimmering without meaning, like the scales of a fish aglow in liquid.

What is it alpha tries to work on? Does dream-work help to shape the big-bang universe? When does the universe begin dreaming itself? Does it dream itself into existence? Does dreaming help shape evolution?

"Jackie"

Jackie, who chronically ruins portions of her life, recently dreamt that her analyst was angry at her, while her old boyfriend, "Mark", prepared a lovely meal for her. In actuality, she made it impossible for her boyfriend to stay. She routinely attacked him for faults and deprecated nourishing aspects. They had intense moments that kept them together for several years, until he could no longer bear the punishment. She kept breaking off with him, and finally he stayed away. He eventually married someone else, apparently happily, while she found another man to feel bad with.

Jackie's therapist consulted me over the years, and I knew how loyal she was to her patient. She stayed through gruelling attacks, break-offs, and the despair of going from bad to worse. My hunch is that Jackie would eat herself alive without therapy. As it was, she came close to vanishing into grisly attack/self-attack spins.

She picked men who were bad for her or whom she chewed to pieces. The wonder was that she had found a therapist who could be good for her. She had been through therapies that were empty or calamitous. Past therapists withdrew, attacked, kicked her out, or she found reasons to make it impossible to stay. Her present therapist stuck it out through thick and thin. She was patient through her own inevitable impatience and held the course through wicked storms.

How did Jackie manage to find a therapist who might endure her? Does this not point to something positive in her that she keeps attacking? Or does she keep attacking what feels bad in herself—as if ripping at herself would destroy the bad thing? Or, perhaps closer, the positive and the bad are fused and indistinguishable, so that by attacking one, she attacks the other. Whether she will destroy her present therapy is not a settled issue.

She achieved some modicum of splitting in her dream, preserving a bit of goodness. At the same time, she put her therapist down: even her old boyfriend was better than her therapist. Nevertheless, her therapist *was* angry and her boyfriend *was* nourishing, as well as the reverse. Shifting mixtures and partitions of anger and nourishment are very real.

Jackie might say something like: "I couldn't take in that Mark was nourishing. My dream makes it clear. When I saw him, I smashed him for not being nourishing enough—not being nourishing at all. There were moments I knew he wasn't as bad as I made out. . . . He was controlling, narcissistic, flawed. But that doesn't mean he didn't give me anything. He gave me whatever he could, and I was biting and couldn't let it in. What was real was the bad stuff—the good stuff didn't make up for it. My dream flashes on the good. I guess it got in somewhere."

The worse life is, the more one appreciates a taste of heaven. I think Jackie let in a bit of Eden, except she could not appreciate it when it was happening. She let it in years afterwards—when it was lost. Why can she do this now? Partly because her therapist is nourishing enough to absorb some anger. She is there enough to allow tolerance for anger–nourishment fusion. The possibility of a nourishing situation absorbing angry elements exists.

With Mark, the situation was too combustible. Her anger fed his, and his fed hers. A potentially nice moment easily became incendiary. They triggered each other off. Each lobbied for his or her own rightness. At the time the break happened, she really was convinced that the failure of their relationship was his fault and that she was the victim of one more bad choice. They could not leave the vortex of the damaged/damaging bond.

Jackie's therapist might feel the pressure of forces involved but does not jump into bad-mouthing brawls. Therapist and patient are not in bed together, spending weekends provoking collapse and mayhem. In therapy a situation gradually grows in which anger does not cancel nourishment and nourishment does not dissolve anger. Facts of emotional life are acknowledged. One can recognize goodness in what one imagined was a bad object, as well as badness in a good object. Jackie's system was making room for both. Her dream recognized a basic goodness that anger does not obliterate.

Abusive rage and tyrannies that marked her childhood form a background that fuses with people to whom she grows close. Intimacy means something bad is going to happen. Nourishment means that trauma is on the way. Trauma is the rule. Nourishment is extracted from injury (see Eigen, 1999).

Wounds become watering-holes. A mother can give and resent giving at the same time, so that what is given is taken away. For Jackie, the situation was even worse. The milk she drank was fused with emotional injury, so that she felt damaged by what kept her alive. Anything enlivening must be damaging. Her boyfriend did not stand a chance. Her therapist understood this, and did not rush her into life. She knew that anything good in their bond was cause for alarm.

Therapy, then, included ingredients the rest of Jackie's life did not. For example, it offered a hint of intimacy that did not push her into anything—a nourisher who understood that nourishment was life-threatening. It is novel to be in a relationship with someone who appreciates the dangers of the relationship as it unfolds yet perseveres respectfully. It is good to be with someone who knows how difficult it is to be with someone, yet how worthwhile it can be.

Therapy included a person who could see the comical aspect of dreaming of an angry therapist and loving boyfriend—a wonderfully precise humour of a dream bent on doing justice to reality by reversing and exaggerating the facts of life, so that the latter might be noticed and appreciated. Dreams often oversimplify to the point of caricature, but they often do so in the service of complexity. Jackie tried to reduce experience to the worst common denominator, but her dream would not let her. Her dream points to goodness that survives the worst.

In response to the dream's goodness, Jackie might say: "What good is all this? Even if I could acknowledge Mark's goodness when we were together, I wouldn't have been different. I'd still lash out. I can't stop it. Even if I know I'm destroying something good, I can't help it. I can understand it comes from my horrible family. What good does that do? I tune into what's wrong with the other person and can't resist. At the time, I feel right. It doesn't matter that I'm destroying something good when I'm attacking something bad. I must attack the bad thing. Nothing you can say makes a difference."

No, nothing her therapist can say, perhaps. But her therapist's attitude, devotion, intermittent persistence, regrouping, seeing—atmospheric intangibles—are not entirely negligible. Does not something of the spirit of the hour seep through and eventually fertilize dream soil? Jackie's dream makes therapy real. At the same time, Jackie's therapy supports processes that make the realization of her dream possible.

Through the walls

Jackie's dream surprises her. To picture her bad boyfriend as good brings her up short. What is her dream doing? What is it telling her? The surprise is made up of a compost of many layers and includes splitting, reversal, fusion, idealization, and distillation.

Splitting.   There is a split between anger and love. Jackie's therapist is angry, her boyfriend is loving, good breast/bad breast.

Reversal.   The dream contains double reversals. Jackie's controlling, withholding, angry, selfish boyfriend is giving and nourishing. Her caring therapist is angry, critical, and accusing. Jackie's view of the predominant state of each is reversed. Someone she views as positive is negative. Someone she views as negative is positive. In truth, she does have a negative attitude towards therapy, as well as a butchered positive sense of her difficult boyfriend. No one is one thing. Tendencies and counter-tendencies coexist.

Fusion.   Anger and nourishment are fused. Jackie's therapist is experienced as nourishing, and it is a basically nourishing figure who is depicted as angry. This is something new. Her dream envisions a nourisher who can include counter-tendencies and not be destroyed. Caring that includes anger goes on being caring. In this context, anger, too, may be nourishing.

There is a reverse fusion in the figure of Jackie's boyfriend. A hated/hating figure is nourishing and loving, so that what seems to be a split is also a fusion. This refers, partly, to the tendency to whitewash a bad object, seeing someone who is bad as better. But it also refers to the need to live out fusions of angry and loving feelings in a relationship. For Jackie, this does not work outside therapy, as angry feelings wreck the good. Affect fusion does not work for Jackie in her life, but she begins to get a taste of it working in therapy.

Idealization.   Jackie unconsciously clings to heaven through hells. Her dream creates an idealized moment with her boyfriend. It may be that unconscious need for idealization increased attacks on him. Perhaps, too, he wanted to be an idealized object for her, and she shattered his narcissism. She felt she attacked badness, but there is also a need to attack goodness to see whether the latter can stand it.

In real life she succeeded in driving her boyfriend away, but her dream recognizes a good, if idealized, core she feared sustaining.

At the same time, idealized moments can spread into a demand that one be treated every moment as if it were a birthday celebration. The need to be idealized, taken care of, and given to can obscure the perception that we are all infinitely precious beings. Nevertheless, whether smeared by idealization or hate, goodness surprises her in her dream.

Distillation. The dream distils basic affect states and situations— in this case, angry and giving feelings. The dream tends to make objects carriers of affects: angry therapist, loving boyfriend. Jackie disowns feelings, projects them into others, and reacts against them. In the dream itself she is strangely neutral, blank, open. She may be a little afraid of her therapist's anger and pleased by her boyfriend's affectionate meal. But her state is somewhat mystified and wide-eyed, as if marvelling that such things can happen. She is more an observer, like an infant gazing at the amazing appearance of things.

Her dreamy passivity is different from her usual attacking self. In intimate situations she tends not to take responsibility for her emotions but attacks the other for not being giving and caring enough. In the dream she is more a seer or be-er than reactor, noting what is rather than obliterating it. The dream distils a function missing in daily life: the ability to attend to what is there rather than walling off and launching missiles at it. The dream passes through her defences, at the same time using aspects of defensive organizations. The dreamer who sees the dream represents an open state of mind she needs more of in daily life, an attitude she scarcely recognizes as possible. My hunch is that the dreamer who sees the dream and does not judge it links up with the therapist's open attitude, ready to let whatever is register.

The possibility of goodness in the world is distilled by placing it squarely in the hands of a derogated object, a lost opportunity. Her old boyfriend, Mark, was not as bad as her parents, not even close, although it seemed so to Jackie at times, until the sense of his badness overwhelmed her. Jackie was dumbfounded by his marriage and reports that he and his wife did not tear each other down all the time, that they had a decent life and were going to be parents. In a way, her dream was a sort of betrayal. How could it show Mark in such a good light and taunt her with his goodness? Did her dream process not know how bad he was? Had her psyche not forced her to fight him? Is this an evil trick played by a dream imp? She defends herself from the bad in him, only to be shown the good too late.

It is difficult for Jackie to feel that the dream could be part of a potential growth process, an invitation to stretch herself. She is tempted to put the dream down, as she was to detonate her lover. What are dreams—psychic noise, part of the cruelty of life, worthless insults, mad gibberish? What do dreams know? What does anyone know? How can a dream stop her from destroying her life? It is difficult to think that the dream might be an outgrowth of the background support provided by therapy, that it could add something to her life—that, indeed, therapy could help her life add up. Will the dream not be swept away by the same rage and dread that killed off all her relationships? Will bad feelings not wreck therapy too?

The dream surprise catches her attention and, like therapy, invites her to pay attention to herself. The implicit message of her dream and therapy is that it and she are worth paying attention to. She may not know what to do with facts of anger and nourishment, but they are part of life needing consideration.

Idealization holds open the possibility of goodness in the dream. In many instances, idealization coats or insulates goodness or acts as the latter's proxy and decoy. In the current dream image, it is linked with a lovely meal and a sense that life is worth living. The therapist absorbs enough rage to leave some room for loving feelings.

Food is to physical nourishment what love is to emotional nourishment. In the dream image, food is part of emotional nourishment, and emotional nourishment is part of feeding. There is givingness in the universe, and it would be less than truthful for Jackie to deny it. In a loving context, food nourishes the emotional self. Indeed, in showing a good meal, the dream is affirming emotional food. In showing a loving boyfriend and an angry therapist, her dream-life gives her something to chew on. Can you take paradoxical images in and make something of them? Can you grow emotionally by seeing things as they are? Can emotional truth be emotional food?

Jackie's dream aims at the unbudgeable in her life, works it over a bit, gives it a twist. Dream-work, once too damaged to do this, tries its hand at reshaping experience. Can she grow into it and let it work on her?

Simultaneity of digestion/evacuation

Bion (1992, pp. 52–68) works with the notion that indigestion is part of digestion. There are variations on this theme, involving (1) the transcendental object (undigested fact); (2) indigestible parts of a digestible fact or object or fact about an object; and (3) evacuative products.

An example of the first two is my mate as an ongoing undigested fact that makes digestion possible. As the years pass, my life with her deepens, yet who she is is not exhausted by who I think she is. As a transcendental object or subject beyond my control and grasp, her personality provides nourishment and support by its very resistance to complete digestibility. I can make of her what I will, and my dreams turn her over and around in various ways, but there is, too, an indigestible core that feeds what digestion my being can manage.

Recurrent pain between us spurs reshaping processes, involving elements of digestion. Moments of peace, joy, or pleasure spread throughout the body of self and are partly digested as well. Over the years I learn to let in both—the "dialectic" of pain and pleasure, collision and renewal. A relationship surviving vicissitudes is akin to Winnicott's (1989) object surviving destruction or Bion's (1970) self moving between fragmentation and security. Deep sweetness makes sourness bearable; at the same time, sourness saves us from blandness and adds seasoning and differentiation. Our cactus needles save us from complete digestibility and dissolution, protect growth, add strength to the sweet core.

In Jackie's case, her therapist and Mark are, partly, undigested, indigestible realities or facts or transcendental objects/subjects. Her dream reverses her core split affect, making her angry boyfriend nourishing and her caring therapist angry, inviting her to grow. It gives her the slightest peek at the object behind the affect. After all, there *is someone* she calls her therapist and *someone* she once called boyfriend. Life forces her to see that he is more or other than she imagined, as her therapist is more too, and as *she* may be more. Who is the being who affects us? Jackie learns that her sour schema will not do justice to all present experience. Her psychic digestive system is wounded. She cannot use nourishment life offers. Yet indigestible aspects of her therapist aid Jackie's digestion. Her therapist's anger awakens awareness that nourishment and mutual respect is possible. A good deal goes on in a relationship that is not usable, difficult, detrimental, but nourishment comes through.

Jackie's dream forces her to notice that the way she sees things is not the only way to see things—that, in fact, the way she thinks she sees things is not the only way *she* does see things. She is more than the sum of what she imagines, as are, too, people she meets. She wishes she could be less imprisoned by whatever turns nourishment into something indigestible and makes something indigestible seem nourishing.

Therapy provides a relationship that lasts through alternative ways of interpreting itself. It is resistant to destruction by the nourishment it provides, and its destructive aspects do not cancel its nourishing possibilities. The fact that therapy *can* be interminable brings home the fact that one does not exhaust what life offers (even if one is exhausted by life) and must grant whatever involves one deeply a measure of transcendence.

Bion raises consciousness of how much experience is not digested or is indigestible. It begins to seem miraculous that we digest anything at all. Yet we give to each other and take in what is offered in many ways. We support each other in life and are supported by life or by something we sense working through life. It is good to realize that there is much to learn about our fragile and resilient digestive process, which span dimensions we call physical, intellectual, emotional, spiritual. It is a relief to realize how little attention we are able to pay to ourselves and things, and how precious attentive moments really are. As Jackie's dream indicates, it is possible that something in us pays attention to our lives very carefully and creates surprising images and scenes with dumbfounding precision, whether or not we are able to pay attention to

it. And even when dream-work is damaged and cannot do its job—
perhaps especially then—it tell us that something is very wrong
that needs attention.

Evacuative eyes

We take the soul of things into our soul through our eyes. This, of
course, is an old thought. Eyes are a kind of mouth, an incorporative organ *par excellence*, the more dramatic because they take in at
a distance. Distance is bridged by spiritual, emotional, and intellectual ingestion—a greater acrobatic feat than swallowing food. The
feat is even more amazing because distance is sustained at the
same time it is bridged. Unlike literal eating, the object remains
outside us as we take it in.

To be sure, the mouth participates in spirit too. It does not eat
dumbly but with taste, discrimination, appreciation. It is alive, and
imaginings are part of its movement. There is a hungry soul or self
or brain or mind that taste, sight, sound, and touch feed. We are
hungry for images that life feeds us, and we work over impressions
incessantly. Dream-work encodes and decodes what happens to us
and is a happening itself. How does our deep dreaming self make
use of all our senses, everything we have seen or heard or
touched—indeed, everything we have imagined? It is easy to understand how the ancients could conceive omniscient intelligence
as part of an All-Soul that ignites our being.

If dream-work is damaged, eyes work in reverse. They expel
rather than take in.

In this case, vision gets rid of emotion rather than imaginally
elaborates, tastes, reworks it. The hallucinatory aspect of dreaming
wraps itself around unprocessable feeling, which is ejected visually
into outside objects. In one scenario, Bion (1992, p. 66) describes the
dream as a kind of containing missile resulting in visual evacuation—a missile container taking emotions further into space or
dispersing them into objects. Instead of ideograms storing and
initiating processing of impacts, vision is exploited to keep feeling
at a distance.

Dream-work, then, functions in opposite ways. It aids in taking
in and processing emotional experience and thus plays an impor-

tant role in memory and attention. It also ejects emotion the person feels unable to bear without rupture. A dream may be more incorporative or more evacuative at any moment and usually is both. If the evacuative aspect is set and chronic, a person may feel that he cannot dream or think or feel. Memory and attention are damaged.

We are challenged to become more sensitive and develop psychic taste buds so that we can sense when a dream is a dream and not a dream, whether it is an attempt to move us along or rid the psyche of itself. By developing our connection to dream-work, we may sometimes sense when a dream is part of a digestive process or symptom of psychic indigestion.

Often it is both. As an indigestible aspect of the object may be needed to further digestion, perhaps an evacuative element is necessary to let us take something in. We expel in order to let in. Letting in too much of anything may be more than we can bear. Evacuation is part of filtration. We push away enough so that letting in is bearable—or, at least, barely bearable.

Evacuation is part of physical digestion—an end-product. In psychological digestion it comes at the beginning and somewhat lets up as processing intake unfolds. We close off and push out more at the outset, in order to open as we can to what is entering us. As absorption goes on, we relax and make the most of what is happening, ready to pull back, shut off, and eject as necessary. Evacuation is part of the regulation of psychic intake.

If dream-work is damaged, evacuation hypertrophies, crippling psychic flow. Emotional processing atrophies, becomes malignant and deformed, or, at best, remains unborn. Dream-work freezes, and personality is crippled with fear and compresses/inflates with hate. Still, moments of processing appear, and if one listens, psychic pulse beats can be heard.

The object that stops dreaming

Bion (1992, pp. 33, 59, 69) writes that dream-work breaks down when what one needs to dream is too terrifying to dream. We try to dream the object that stops dreaming. The undreamable object draws on multiple sources.

1. From the beginning of life, emotional growth was not sup-
    ported in a way that made effective dream-work possible. For
    dream-work to evolve, it would have to process this lack of
    support and dream what damaged it—exactly what it cannot,
    dare not do. This is one reason why Bion feels that nightmares
    are an achievement. Some aspect of horror has been sustained,
    enough to wake the person up and, momentarily, link conscious
    and unconscious fear.

2. Dread that stops dreaming does not need magnification but
    undergoes magnification anyway. We infinitize dreads. Trau-
    matizing objects become imaginal/hallucinatory nuclei. Bad as
    they are, they become boundless: a witch or devil, not only
    ghastly mother, father, or self. What frightens one is unimagina-
    ble, and devils glimpsed are contracted nibbles. Our muscula-
    ture and perhaps nervous system tighten in pain and remain
    knotted all through life, fused with visual terror.

3. The object that stops dreaming is encoded as frightening super-
    ego. Here superego has a menacing quality, without a frame of
    reference to circumscribe it. It is akin to what Bion (1965; Eigen,
    1996) describes as a force that goes on working after it destroys
    personality, time, and existence. Can one imagine a destructive
    force that has, as its full time employment, the destruction of
    whatever it can destroy? It aims at any life-producing moment,
    so that whatever bit of aliveness manages to surface is subject
    to attack.

We are using words here to point to something nonverbal or trans-
verbal: a boundless destruction that inspires attempts to express it,
yet damages apparatus necessary for such attempts.

What can therapy offer? Therapists, among other things, may
be auxiliary dream-workers who support personality in order to let
dream-work dream. We enable people to dream the undreamable
and draw growth-stopping damage into dream-work that connects
one with oneself. Dream-work is steeped in infinite heartbreak
and terror, but there are, too, infinities of beauty that break the
heart, like bread, in joy, which dream-work tastes, chews, digests,
celebrates, crumb by crumb.

CHAPTER FOUR

The undreamable object

B ion (1992) proposes the notion of an object so frightening that it cannot be dreamt—an object that stops dreaming. The dreads we know are hints of dreads we do not, perhaps cannot, know. The dread of dreads is a kind of negative counterpart to the Kabbalistic *Ein Sof*, God as unknown infinite, infinite of infinites. Only here it is God in utmost negative aspect, destroyer rather than bringer of life (see or touch God and die, see Medusa and die). Bion proposes the notion of a dread of dreads that is not only unnameable, but also undreamable.

To be undreamable is to be unprocessable. For Bion, dreams are critical for processing, "digesting", or making use of experience.

> Dream-work is responsible for rendering pre-communicable material "storable" and communicable; the same for stimuli and impressions derived from the contact of the personality with the external world. Contact with reality is *not* dependent on dream-work; accessibility to the personality of the material derived from this contact *is* dependent on dream-work. [Bion, 1992, p. 45]

Bion places a great weight on dreaming, dream-work, and the capacity to use dreams:

> The failure of dream-work and the consequent lack of avail-ability of experience of external or internal psychic reality gives rise to the peculiar state of the psychotic who seems to have contact with reality but is able to make singularly little use of it either for learning from experience or for immediate consumption. [Bion, 1992]

Dream-work is involved with the storage of impacts of experience and renders contact with inner/outer reality usable. Bion depicts a state of affairs (called psychotic) in which contact with inner/outer reality is possible, but not usable. One neither learns from nor is nourished by this contact. In some crucial way, experience fails to build on itself.

One cannot gain access to one's own experience. Results of contact with reality (inner/outer) are not accessible to personality. As suggested in chapter three, dream-work supports and feeds personality. Damaged dream-work is akin to short-circuiting the personality's oxygen or food supply. What causes failure of dream-work or damaged dream-work? What enables dream-work to be relatively successful?

Bion suggests that our very drive for psychophysical nourish-ment is projected into the other, that it needs support from the other for sustenance. Aggressive, dependent, and creative "drives" find their way into the other's insides, and what happens with the former depends partly on what happens in the latter. The notion that we are dependent on what happens to us in another person leads into a field of experience that requires careful atten-tion.

First, some disclaimers. I am well aware of the objection that Klein–Bion are speaking of the infant's phantasy of "putting" its insides into another's insides or seeing in the other bits of oneself without realizing it. Nevertheless, I have heard Bion say that the effects of putting oneself in another are quite real. Effects of phan-tasy are very real. Moreover, as biological beings, we seek what we need from the environment and phantasy helps motivate, direct, and modulate our activity.

Bion, amplifying Klein, tracks annihilating dreads the infant puts into the mother's being and mental work the mother does on the former. The mother's "reverie" of the baby and what the baby "makes" her feel affect her state of being, and so the baby's. It seems like saying 2 + 2 = 4 to say that how the mother sees the baby affects the baby. The mother's mental state impacts on the baby's state of being. If the mother makes room for the baby's dread of destruction and modulates it through responsiveness, the baby gains a sense that life survives agonizing fears. As time goes on, agonizing terrors take their places in an emotional frame of reference that includes but goes beyond them.

But what if the baby is thrown back on itself, meets a wall, or more anxiety or hostility? What if, to use Bion's locution, the object is intolerant of projective identification? What if the caregiver cannot let the baby's feelings affect her or reacts destructively? What if the worst a baby can feel cannot get into another person for modification or psychic reworking? What if the other person refuses the input, evacuates it, cannot bear it, or does not have equipment to process it? What if the baby's feelings have nowhere or very hurtful places to go? [Winnicott (1989) also focuses on what happens if one's sense of aliveness has nowhere to go or gets damaged; in *Toxic Nourishment* (1999) I explore this theme in ways that connect with the work presented here.]

One thing that gets projected into the object is the baby's object-seeking drives. The very urge to be with another enters the other, seeks another to go into and be a part of. One goes into another to create a response, to have a place in another person, to be part of someone's life. One needs the other's thoughts and feelings for one's own psychic nourishment. This level of interpenetration is deeper than issues of control. We may, also, wish to get inside the other in order to manipulate the latter. But the primordial in–in flow, in which the other's mind and being and psyche are necessary to house my own, is not fundamentally manipulative. It simply is.

If the projecting personality cannot hit pay dirt, it cannot develop. It may stagnate, grow in warps, suffer deformation. Life goes on in strangulated, sometimes determined ways. One may become passive or die out, but one may also (perhaps in circumscribed ways) become a monster. In everyday living, our monster selves often baffle us, interacting in seamless ways with our benign and well-formed aspects. By the time we awaken to ourselves, we have an entrenched sense of being excluded/included with regard to the desire of others, partly as a result of whether and how we found our way inside another and what became of us there.

In order for object-seeking feelings to thrive, or even feel real, they have to be projected into another who works with them. The drive to make contact with the other needs to find the other's insides and stimulate thought, feeling, imagining. One needs to feel who one is elaborated in the mind of another. This is a little like the mother bird beginning the digestive process for the baby, only here we are speaking about the transmission and digestion of feelings involved with one's sense of being.

One way of saying this is that the therapist needs to dream the patient. The patient has to make his way into the therapist's dreamwork, and the therapist not only has to let this happen but has to enable it or move with it. In one passage Bion writes: "Anxiety in the analyst is a sign that the analyst is refusing to 'dream' the patient's material: not (dream) = resist = not (introject)." (Bion, 1992, p. 43). That is, the analyst is not letting the patient affect him in the place where dreams form. Freud speaks of a dream navel— an enigmatic dream centre or point where the dream forms, its roots in the unknown, images like branches we swing on before they break or we let go. There are some patients who cannot get the feel of themselves or move on unless they feel they have seeped through the therapist's dream navel into the unknown, and that what the therapist says or does grows out of the unknown depths, filters through the dream navel into images, gestures, statements.

It may be that a patient needs to be dreamt by an analyst before the former can make use of dreaming. He may need an experience of becoming a useful part of another's dream-work before getting the feel of using his own. He may actually have to feel the other's alpha function working on him—mother bird pre-digesting him, ready to feed him to himself. He may not be able to digest himself or use his own processes until he gets the feel of another doing it with him. The analyst, at such moments, may be a kind of auxiliary alpha function or primary processor or dream-worker. The patient learns for himself that such a possibility exists, senses it, begins to get the knack himself. Without such an experience, the patient may have felt deeply undreamable and so shut out of the heart of life.

It can be an important step to discover oneself a deeply dreamable object.

It emboldens one to allow others into one's own dream navel, to be used for growth. But what if one fails to be a dreamable object? What if one remains an object that cannot be dreamt? What if one is so frightening to oneself that one becomes an object that stops dreaming?

What if one covers oneself with a fright that cannot be dreamt in order to hide from an intimation of an even more frightening object—an intimation that has undergone a prolonged wiping-out process? What if one has not been part of another's dream, or not part of a good dream, or only part of a bad dream? What if one's sense that one is inedible and indigestible coats a damaged or blank sense of another too horrible to let in? What if one's ghastly self is a quasi-image of another one cannot look at?

To summarize so far: we seek. We seek someone to project ourselves into. We seek someone who will let us in, dream us, make us part of his or her depths and reverie, someone who will think about and have feelings for us, so that her/his unconscious waking thinking contributes to our sense of self. Winnicott (1989) refers to a time when the infant and mother are a kind of unit, so that the mother's state of being is part of the infant and *vice versa*. What happens if one or the other rejects or cannot enter into such a unit or enters into it in deforming ways? Because of our permeability, we do affect one another, and our refusal or deformation of this flow is, also, part of mutual impact.

Seeking and projecting go together. Seeking is part of the projecting personality (Bion, 1992, p. 35). Seeking and projecting constitute a kind of drive to communicate self and touch reality. One reaches into outer space to find the inner space of another person. The image of sending signals into space in the hope that our messages will be met applies to what happens in fast motion between ourselves moment to moment. We try to communicate our capacity to communicate at the same time as we attempt to communicate ourselves.

At times, self-to-self transmission connects, and faith in communication grows. Often difficulties stimulate struggle and effort, resulting in partial communication, enough to make attempts at further communication worthwhile. We partly let each other in, partly get each other's attempts to communicate. Mutual correction and nuanced approximation become part of our way of life. Nevertheless, there are times when a ghastly result of self signals being unmet, sent back unanswered or deformed, is that a mad part of personality, hostile to communication, grows where communication might have been. This is different from regrouping after communication failure to try again. When projective identification comes up against an intolerant object as personality forms, the very attempt to communicate can become persecuting.

Bion formulates the turning of communicative capacity against itself in various ways, and I am not trying to be exhaustive here. (Aspects of Bion's formulations involving the personality's attempt to cancel itself can be found in Eigen, 1986, 1996, 1998, 1999.) In the passages (Bion, 1992, pp. 34–36) where tropism = seeking = projective identification seeking nourishment (i.e. seeking alpha function or dream-work of the other), the object's intolerance of projective identification results in the personality (1) introjecting intolerance of communication ("a peculiar form of primitive superego hostile to projective identification even as a method of communication, and so, by extension, to all forms of communication") and (2) partial reintrojection of the tropism "enclosed within the vehicle of communications itself, be that sound, sight, or touch. Thus enclosed, the tropism and its envelope become persecuted and persecuting" (Bion, 1992, p. 35).

In this picture, there are multiple forms of persecution going on simultaneously within the personality. The self takes in the object's intolerance of self, and an inner persecuting "superego" aims against object-seeking tendencies. Further, the process of communication grows around itself, encapsulating and deforming the wish to communicate. Communication becomes, in a way, its negative counterpart, a destructive urge to undo all possibility of communication. This puts the personality in the untenable position of stimulating a force that destroys communication each time communication is attempted (Eigen, 1999).

To represent such an annihilating force or object would be to represent an object that destroys representation. One may need another's help to do this, but the ability to avail oneself of help may be compromised. If the truth of one's life is that the capacity for communication has been destroyed or stunted, one would be hard put to make use of another's alpha function/dream-work, although that may be what is needed in order to restore one's own.

In other words, the ability to seek another or seek oneself has to be projected into another and met by alpha function/dream-work in order for life-seeking tendencies to be sustained, softened, and utilized for growth. A person may come for help because elemental projective attempts turned to stone, became mutilated, encapsulated, partly murdered, or worn out. In many, partial annihilation of self is depicted in nightmares. There are individuals for whom having a nightmare is a step forward. A nightmare, at least, is able to image a bit of the terror that freezes psychic processing. It represents a portion of what cannot be represented before breaking apart (nightmares usually destroy themselves as dreams, awakening the dreamer).

Bion notes that an entire session or part of a session may be an attempt by an individual to dream the dream that cannot be dreamt, the *necessary* dream. The tone or atmosphere or spirit of sessions may be informed by the object that prevents or undoes dream-work. The analyst is in the position of maintaining sufficient alpha function/dream-work to jump-start that of the patient in the face of pressures that annihilate or vastly compromise psychic work (Bion, 1992, p. 33). To learn to use one's psyche is more difficult than it is for a child to learn to walk, if psychic "muscles" are atrophied, missing, or malformed. The analyst must support the patient in the face of disability, as ability slowly grows.

Bion repeatedly refers to fear of a murderous superego as a shorthand way of communicating the terror/hate that prevents the formation and use of alpha function/dream-work. In a sense, one is afraid to come together as a person because that would entail emergence of the terrifying superego. Bion is especially concerned with the instance in which the alpha function/dream-work that would support coming together as a person is damaged—and that it can only go forward by dreaming what is damaging the capacity to dream. Suppose one were blind, and the only way to gain vision were to stare wide-eyed into an eclipse that would, in turn, damage the capacity to see. Bion delineates an extreme instance in which the ability to put together anything is akin to putting together the terrifying superego that damages alpha function/dream-work (Bion, 1992, p. 33).

In semi-Kleinian terms, fear of assembling the object that damages alpha function/dream-work prevents use of the Positions:

> the patient's fear of the murderous super-ego prevents his approaching the Positions [paranoid-schizoid and depressive positions]. This in turn means he is unable to dream, for it is in dream that the Positions are negotiated. He therefore postpones this experience till the analytic session in which he hopes he will have support, or perhaps, feeling he has support, dares to have the dream he cannot have without consciousness of support. [Bion, 1992, p. 37]

I say "semi-Kleinian" because Bion is concerned with damage so pervasive that the individual is afraid or unable to utilize primary process/alpha function/dream-work. He is even afraid or unable to use projective identification—which is, for Klein, a primal psychic operation and basic building block. Bion sees splitting, projection, and introjection as a part of dream-work, together with displacement, condensation, juxtaposition, and the like. Klein's paranoid-schizoid (splitting/projection) and depressive (introjection) positions are, in part, ways in which alpha function works: taking apart, putting together, projecting out, taking in.

Bion may be pulling on a thread Klein took for granted. But I am not sure that Klein aimed at or saw the point where projection (seeking) was so totally in jeopardy. Bion hits a sore spot where projection is stuck or stillborn. Bits of projection that manage to survive depict damage—not only damaged self and personality, but damaged projective ability, hints of what damaged it, and a sense of what makes its use damaging. In such a state, to use projection is to simulate annihilation, or worse. I think Bion tips Klein over the edge by plunging the psyche into a field of continuous annihilation, so that to exercise the capacity to dream annihilation represents an enormous achievement. Bion makes it clear that a sense of environmental support is necessary to move towards dreaming—that is, unless the dream is simply part of the annihilating field and not an attempt to note, record, and begin delineating it.

What makes perception of environmental support possible when (1) seeking is damaged; (2) there is a gravitational pull towards the damaging object; (3) one expects to see or find the damaging object if one sees and finds anything at all? There are only partial "answers" to questions like these. One factor is whether or not environmental support is actually there. Is the analyst's alpha function/dream-work at the patient's disposal for constructing the necessary dream? To what extent is the analyst too damaged, distant, or clinging for the necessary work to take place? Is the analyst's psyche actually available for work to be done?

My sense is that over time nourishing aspects of the environment do get through (often osmotically): (1) if one does not totally succumb to the gravitational pull of damaging-object/damaged capacity; (2) if real nourishing aspects outlast or co-exist with damaging aspects. Insofar as the possibility of nourishment is there, the possibility of someone noticing it may increase. Partly, it is a matter of mutual endurance, long-term interpenetration of nourishing/ anti-nourishing forces, gradual shifts of balance.

This may seem like too great a burden to place on an analyst and, in fact, it is. In many instances, extra-analytic help is as important as or more important than analytic nourishment. But often a person fails to make enough use of the former without help from the latter.

"Milton"

Milton (Eigen, 1999, Ch. 4) spoke of the film title, *Eyes Wide Shut*. He had not seen the movie, just advertisements. "I'll see it", he said. "As soon as I heard the title, I thought Kubrick must know what I feel; eyes open but not seeing." Milton described going through life like that. Eyes open—not seeing. His eyes could not see because they were frozen in terror. Terror and rage were one. Apparently, Milton intuited that the film was concerned with damaged dream-work and the need to repair.

Milton had much body therapy. In a way, his body was his eyes. He could see deep within his body. But his body saw only one thing: "White contempt lives inside me, hate mostly, poison, my living reality. My body is black inside—an abiding, enduring state of affairs. Nothing else but the coherence of this hate." This hate was also terror.

Milton rarely brought dreams into therapy. Each session was a ghastly dream—a dream of hate–terror in which everything that happened in the session was indistinguishable from the hate–terror his body was. The room was a body filled with hate–terror, a frozen room, a room that could not change. I was part of this body, but also (hopefully) witness to it. My role was something like Horatio's, to bear witness to the ghastliness with painful breath; to say, yes, Milton's story is real, what he endures exists. My role is like a witness to the Holocaust: never forget. My role is to let others know, to somehow connect Milton with his own knowledge, to dare to believe the unbelievable.

Love exists in Milton's life, but he cannot experience it, he cannot let it build in a way that he can feel and say yes to, a way that counts for him. How do I know love exists in Milton's life? He is a totally dedicated father, husband, worker. He is devoted to the people in his life. He cares about getting it right, giving it his best. He works hard at every aspect of his life. He works hard at therapy. There is deep love in his kind of devotion and caring. Milton admits that this is true . . . must be true. Love must be part of his nature. But the truth is—and I must get this right—there is an area of self—the area that counts most to Milton, the place he lives, the place he truly is—where no love is. There is a point that is his very sense of reality, the sense of feeling real/unreal, where no love penetrates. Milton's truth of truths.

His children are precious to him, his wife is also precious; his work is deeply valued, deeply meaningful. But what rivets his attention is the place of terror–hate that condenses into a voice that mocks, puts down, sees the Achilles heel in everything, the place where only the devil is real. Everyone must have this fear–terror. Everyone must be this devil too. Surely, living from any other place must be phoney, as long as the sea of terror exists. Only evil is real—which means that nothing is real.

It is a little like Descartes going on with life as usual while everything is subject to radical doubt, going on with love and work, as they are nulled, poisoned, fall through the eternal trap-door. The point Milton wants us to know is that he has fallen through that door and speaks to us from the fall. Does this mean that he partly assumes that we are not falling too? That we are and are not real? That he is and is not real? Has a note of ambivalence, doubt crept in, doubt about his doubt? Does something, indeed, exist besides the univocal nulling process, ubiquitous hell?

He shouts over and over that everything is agony, unreal, hate, terror—this is what life boils down to. This is not just a rant. It is the place that must be met, the place that gainsays all else and holds sway. If he cannot change this, life will be spoiled. And, moreover, he does not see how this spoiling will not seep into others. What poisons him will poison those close to him and all he touches. It will poison therapy and render me useless.

What Milton learned from the earliest age was that our deepest links and bonds are damaging, damaged, poisoned, poisonous. What bonds us most to life deforms us. He has brought this deforming bond into therapy. Therapy has, to some extent, become versions of it but fails because, so far, it cannot be deformed enough. Something escapes the deforming process and keeps outside the undreamable dream. Damage has not been able to glut itself enough on therapy.

Perhaps my sense of an undamaged x is delusional, desperate negativism in the face of Milton's relentless sense of damage. His need for total damage smokes out my faith in an undamaged point of self, a surviving idealism. How can damage and corruption be everywhere, yet a point of purity remain? Mystical vision of an incorruptible soul point connected with God in the midst of corruption gives pause for reflection and discovery. If something in me partly affirms this incorruptible point, will I drive Milton even crazier? How can he rest before every vestige of denial is torn away?

Milton cannot stop speaking about his deep father and mother wounds. He feels wounded from the beginning of life—born into wounding force fields. His mother was beautiful, drugged, out of it, flickering in and out of reality, in bed much of the time. She could not take care of herself, much less of a baby.

His father took Milton away from his mother in middle childhood. At first, Milton felt saved, but new problems mounted. His father had no trouble getting out of bed, but he was not at home much. He expected Milton to be forever grateful for the sacrifice he made. He expected Milton to worship him. If Milton was victimized by his mother's morass, he was now victimized by his father's egoism. From wound to wound. As Milton grew, he felt the two environments very much parts of him. He found himself sinking in the swamp that covered him from birth and falling on the cutting sword of his father, the tainted, shining knight. He tried to affirm life in the face of anti-life tendencies, but deep inside the latter felt more real.

Soon enough, he saw through his father's self-deceptions, the ways he cheated and got by in order to build himself up and make a living. Milton, at first forgiving, turned merciless within. He missed nothing, perfectly attuned to every nuance of his father's self-aggrandizing gestures. Milton's mind or inner eye became a knife (sharper than his father's), cutting through false moves of self. In a way, integrity was the most real thing in Milton's life—for he felt keenly the lack of it everywhere.

Milton condemned nearly everyone and everything, spotting some failure of integrity, the fatal flaw. Perhaps, after all, condemnation was the most real thing. But condemnation's roots sank deep in wounds, swamps, slashes, lost in prehistory. Milton lashed out at a degraded sense of self with little relief. He could not make the bad feeling go away. He could not make history go away.

His psychic eyes riveted on damage and never let up. Sessions became a place he could trace the damage with all his might, follow where it led, if it led anywhere. Its location changed, belly, heart, head, bowels—it was everywhere. It refused to be pinned down. Yet he followed it, challenged it, fought it, embraced it, went into it, stayed with it.

Our sessions became a place to dream the undreamable dream, to live the pain that cannot be lived.

There were periods of little distinction between shattered self and shattered/shattering object. Milton would try to "ground" (his term) himself in face of the shatter, but often the ground shattered too. Yet each session he started at square one, aiming at ground zero, the point of cataclysm. Whatever he saw and felt was a taste of what he could not see and feel, and he kept stretching—a snake with infinite elasticity expanding around infinitely expanding shatter. Can the infinitely shattering self-and-object ever be encompassed?

Bion's "terrifying superego" is a stand-in for ever more formless damage, a way to stop the bleeding, to congeal fright for a time. One substitutes an undreamable object for an even more sleepless state of affairs. One dare not have a psyche, if psyche itself is absolute horror. Yet this is precisely what Milton tries to brave. He tries to constitute what he can of himself in face of the terror that obliterates his efforts. Our sessions are where he stalks his prey, the desolation that subtends him, only to be beaten down by wave after wave of what he finds.

And where is my alpha function/dream-work? Is it of any use at all? Much of the time it is put out of play. The shattering that Milton addresses cannot be wished away, played down, or placated. It can only be met by truth. Yet it resists my attempts at processing—possibly because there is not enough truth in me. Still, session after session I join Milton in suffering. I feel what he must go through but can do little. He pierces my responses in an instant. There are moments when something gets through to him, some bit of good will or truth. Most often he undoes it at the next meeting, but traces remain.

If I can do nothing else, I can acknowledge the reality of the obliteration that Milton lives. I can do this on many fronts. First, more congealed, rigid, "stabilized" structures: the attacker and attacked. This includes the inner eye that dismantles falsehood, an inner hound following deception's scent. The entire adult world is unmasked, and the phoneyness of life stands guilty as charged.

But heat-seeking missiles go further, seeking the burning child within, and the primal parents, long turned to scar tissues and ashes. Explosion after explosion, and the burning continues. Still, we are only at another portal of obliteration.

The very background of psychic life is damaged. Not only are there dreadful objects that cannot reach dreams, but there is no place to dream them. The dream screen, long in flames, is unusable. It is past the point of warp, although warp persists. Even if something could find its way to dreaming, it would immediately be damaged by the wounded process dreaming has become and by the charred space it needs to project an image.

But is my noting this not a bit of alpha function? Is dream-work not working, if I can write this down, if I say it now? Is this chapter not a kind of waking dream, a little waking unconscious thinking? So alpha function/dream-work, however meagre, does go on. And if it goes on anywhere, there is a chance someone will be nourished.

Milton's sessions are a stalking ground for the undreamable, the unprocessable destruction that never stops destroying. To think of containing it is ridiculous, beyond any capacity I possess. But I glimpse it nonetheless and feel what is at stake. Milton brings us to the edge of something we dare not hide for ever.

To some extent, alpha function/dream-work deals with tendencies that expel alpha function/dream-work. This is part of daily bread. But there are deeper difficulties. Milton has reached a place (or no-place) where he cannot expel horror. Space has been traumatized so that passage is impossible. Horror collapses in on itself, and no alpha function can keep up with it. Experiencing alpha function/dream-work's insufficiency is a start. As I often say, something gets through, something changes.

Milton's sessions may, partly, be a fragment of a dream, or incipient dream, of what he undergoes in the sessions. Even the shatter of a session may be a bit of a dream of shatter too. An aspiration: to undergo and dream what one is undergoing at the same time. Milton will surely slice me if I make a false move, if I have a false hope. It must be the real thing. And the real thing again.

PART TWO

WORK IN THE TRENCHES

CHAPTER FIVE

Cameras

We have always been fascinated with images of ourselves. We now possess little boxes that provide images of ourselves and each other on demand. In view of the camera, we are potential, portable images. We always were, insofar as we viewed each other in our minds. But to be able to produce, nearly instantaneously, images of ourselves that we can hold, pass around, and look at together—such a capability cannot fail to impact upon our sense of self.

When I was a child at school, teachers revelled in stories about "natives" fearing that their souls could be captured by mirror images. A camera, even more than a mirror, was a kind of soul box. Associations of theft, imprisonment, and pictures are seen in terms like "capture": capturing experience, expression, gesture, reality.

As a child, I could not capture in words the muted thrill that went with the conquistador's superiority, the "native's" stupefaction. Not only control of weaponry, but control of soul images— was that not something to marvel at? Not only my own growth lay ahead, but the agonized growth of social consciousness in general.

Within a couple of decades, the cultural climate was such that any group could call into question the superiority of any other group, along any conceivable line (e.g. social, racial, sexual, economic). The categories, above/below, more/less, were suspect.

The days when one group could enjoy stupefying another were over in theory. The thrill of imagining Europeans frightening/ fascinating "natives" with the latter's own images—the image of British and European omniscience establishing dominance over "lower-level" cultures: concentration camps and atom bombs, brutal tips of persistent tumult—ended any era of smug moral superiority for any known class of humanity. Horrifying images of piles of emaciated bodies and peeling skin made it indelibly clear that, yes, we are the kinds of creatures that can do these things to one another. And, yes, we do these things to each other today and tomorrow.

I was nine years old when the Second World War ended. My camera meant freedom to me. I took pictures of family and friends. When I was 13, Dorothy Kirsten sang in my hometown, and my pictures conveyed something of how I felt when the tops of her breasts filled out when she breathed in. The same year, I took a picture of FDR's bust in Hyde Park (New York) that looked ghost-like. Neighbourhood girls helped me to print photos in the dark-room I built in my basement.

It has taken years to get a sense of what it was like growing up during the war. So much infiltrates and registers yet takes years to develop in the darkroom within. A sense of war going on some-where else creates a kind of veil. It creates a temptation to feel that war is for others, a hideous temptation that steals you from your-self. Deep down, you know that you are part of a group that does bloodcurdling things, you are a person, and treating people hor-ribly is something people do.

Life in the school-yard was tough enough, bloody fights erupt-ing you never knew when. If you were lucky, you learned to slip through cracks. Let the tyrannosauruses collide. Deep down, you knew that there was a connection between the school-yard and the battlefield. But you could not imagine Japanese organs undergoing monstrous deformations, or that anyone would do what they did to fellow Jews. This you saw in pictures that changed the way you saw yourself. Could one ever see a human being totally free of gas chambers and the smell of burning flesh? Such realities threaten to break out, like plagues, at any moment.

Years later, as a psychotherapist, I found that cameras appeared in the dreams of my psychotic patients. They appeared in other patients' dreams too: dreaming of cameras does not mean that you are psychotic. But after the decimated or barren landscapes, butchered meat, bloody flowers, frightening attackers—sooner or later, as recovery is under way—cameras.

There are negative and positive meanings one could attach to cameras—but when the latter appear as part of a process of recovery, the positive is emphasized first. Many recovering psychotics not only dream of cameras but go through a phase of actual picture-taking, as if the camera were, for a time, a bridge to reality. The camera becomes a way to check what is—and, more importantly, is not—there. For the moment, there is an image that is not flooded by "something else".

For a time, the camera becomes an extension and activator of the objectifying mind. There is danger of being trapped between flooding and detachment. One may be so relieved to be resurfacing that one holds on to surfaces for dear life. One may try to use photographic images to exclude the mythic and fantastic. "Look, you see—there is an external world after all, and I am part of it." Some individuals go too far and may succeed in squeezing out hints of feeling from their images. The external world becomes a succession of events without insides, without spirit.

More often, photographs assure the individual the world is there and she is in it. What appears has claim to validity and has expressive value. Photographic images are not dissolved by spirit, nor bereft of fantasy. One person I worked with brought in, for a time, images of trees, flowers, barns, landscapes, and collections of objects that contained hints of supernatural beings. You might think you were looking at a tree, but if you kept looking, you began to see the face of a witch or demon or gnome in its curls of branches or knotted bark. The photo contained supernatural forces—fear with a smile.

My patient knew well the terror she toyed with—it was not a thing of the past, over and done with. But for the evil to impishly shape itself in crevices of pictures was an achievement to be proud of. She was well on the way to interacting with forces that shaped her—so that *she* experienced the joy of being a lively part of reshaping processes. With camera in hand, total paralysis lifted.

Even so, the colours and expressions one sees in psychosis rarely appear in pictures. Some individuals, especially in the early phases of breakdown, see colours more intensely than their photographs can show. There will always be some discrepancy between what one perceives in psychosis and what one sees in photographs. To some extent, the difference is frustrating—one cannot capture one's madness in photographs—not fully, purely. But the difference is also reassuring—since world and life and self survive madness.

Sometimes a person feels nostalgia and fear of loss as his psychotic episode lifts. One man told me of colours saturating experience—the world was alive with colour and light, darkness in clouds glistened richly. Before his madness, he did not know that such colour existed. A painter like Turner comes close but, still, there is no more than a hint. Similarly, devils one sees in faces—one really does see devils—no picture conveys this dread, this hellish severity. In pictures, most devils look a little silly. One takes pictures to reassure oneself there is more to life than devils.

Pictures are important because of what does not appear in them. Devils leap out of actual faces, not out of photographs. Devils fall behind a picture, subtend it, lurk around it. This may be akin to the belief that you cannot see the devil's face in a mirror. But we learn from pictures of concentration camps and Hiroshima that photos can show worse things than devils. There are public evils that are far worse than private madness.

A person may feel that the colours seen in madness can sanctify the world and may even pray that the goodness of colour is more fundamental than demonic horror. There is something irreducibly private about the colours one sees while mad. Sometimes one needs to go mad to find the unshareable, sanctifying source.

What is important in photographs, to the individual coming through psychosis, is that they present, salvage, and affirm aspects of the world as such. This is so even if the shared reality grimly eclipses private demons, although photos usually present the presence of the world in relative safety. "I look at someone in a photo with less fear than I dare in person", a man confided.

"I took pictures of my father last week", he continued. "I've been staring at them all weekend. I cry when I see him in photos. I'm angry when I see him in person. In my photos I can see his whole life. I imagine when he was starting out, fresh with youth. I can feel everything life promised. In my photos I see him ageing. He looks at me and smiles. I can feel his smile because I am not with him. I do not have to tighten, to shut him out. I see his smile now—in the pictures. It goes inside me. I can feel his life, the passing of time, and weep. There is so much love in the heart of hearts. So much sadness. So much joy. But when we're together, I stiffen. Something happens, and I can't stand him."

Often pictures let one feel what one cannot feel face to face. One gets a feel of a life, the passage of a life. One gets a sense of time. When the man above saw his father next, there was something mellower, fuller, even though stiff fury remained. The father's vulnerability was more visible, together with caring and regret—the impossibly human mixture of wishing it could have been better, the all too real mixture of poison and purity, joy, reconciliation, ineptitude.

Pictures are important for what they show and what shines through them. They exhibit a slice of life, present an object or a face or a body that says, "I exist. I'm real. I'm radiance. I'm me." In photographs death, too, speaks to the radiance of life, testifying to the realness and value of a moment in time, even a moment in time gone wrong. As my patients recover, their photographs, above all, witness bare "isness", the momentous, ineffable fact that something is at all.

Many things happen in recovery processes. Often a patient generates situations that overwhelm the therapist. Patients sometimes want to take pictures of the therapist. There are therapists who can tolerate this and those who cannot. Many who cannot have a good rationale. They are interested in helping the patient to learn about what motivates the wish, so that the patient can grow in freedom with regard to what moves her. To enact the wish (e.g. patient and therapist having sex or never seeing each other again) robs the patient of the opportunity to experience and study it.

My formulation is incomplete and misleading, since it may not be a matter of can and cannot. There are therapists who do not wait long enough to enable a situation to convert from impending action to study. A therapist may act impulsively or be unable to let the pressure mount. There are, also, therapists who could tolerate picture-taking but choose not to for valid reasons. Some may permit an enactment, then study it. Some may believe that the enactment itself has value. So many permutations, gradations, shades of possibility vie for recognition. Therapy is in the predicament of having a background of conflictual generalities to draw on, while *this* situation with *this* patient and therapist is happening only now.

"Pam" and "Marge"

Marge sought supervisory help because she was overwhelmed by her patient's insistence on taking pictures of her. When Marge, at first, refused, Pam found ways of suddenly whipping out her camera and taking photographs, sometimes on her way out the door or at unexpected moments. Pam was amazing at sensing moments when Marge's guard was down—and out came the camera.

Marge's prior supervision tended to intensify the power struggle between her patient and herself. Her supervisor tried to help Marge to maintain a formal yet friendly setting that could not permit picture-taking but aimed to focus on Pam's state of mind—all her ideas and feelings and what the urge to take Marge's picture was trying to achieve. Marge agreed that limit setting was critical for therapy to be effective, yet her sense of helplessness and violation mounted. She lacked the resources to maintain the desired boundaries. Whatever resources she mustered broke down.

Nevertheless, Marge could not help feeling that the situation was more complex than a simple power struggle. She was in conflict about what to do and, as time went on, became afraid of supervision. Supervision seemed to make the situation worse and, she gradually became aware, following good supervisory lines went against some of her most basic feelings for her patient. She felt caught between betraying supervision or betraying her patient.

There is no recourse in such a situation other than intensifying the journey of self-discovery. Marge consulted me in the hope of opening possibilities beyond what she, her supervisor, and patient were stuck in. Psychoanalytic work was not turning out to be anything like she imagined. Her patient was becoming her worst nightmare. Yet she, in truth, loved her patient.

Marge was caught between love of analysis—she knew at first hand what it could do—and love of her patient. Psychoanalysis is, among other things, a method of exploration. But it is necessary to reinvent or re-envision psychoanalysis according to the requirements of a particular situation. What is at issue is not simply growth or variation of method, but evolution of psychoanalytic intuition itself. Psychoanalysis is only as alive as a practitioner's intuition in a given predicament.

Is it possible to do justice to all aspects of Marge's conflict? No, we do not know what "all" is. But it is somewhat possible to begin letting Marge's agonies and pleasures say what they can and listen. Marge did not want to ruin therapy. She feared ruining it either by losing the integrity of the work or by being too "severe" with Pam (or being perceived as too severe). She wanted neither to compromise the value of the work nor lose the patient. At the centre of feeling frustrated, fearful, furious, and helpless was a sense of violation.

Since the sense of violation was most alive, I asked Marge to speak from it. Different sorts or levels of violation quickly poured out. The crust was anxiety and guilt with regard to the supervisory superego or analytic ideal: what analysis and an analyst *should* be like, or what one imagines therapy *should* be. Her training, experience as a patient, and professional status were being challenged. This *should* is by no means superficial. It touches her personal experience as a patient and the validity of her own personal analysis. Analysis gave her much—it even resulted in giving her a calling. She has a deep sense of loyalty to her patienthood and the way her analyst worked with her. Without quite realizing it, she was expecting to be like her analyst, and her patients to be like her. It is a difficult but important learning experience for an analyst to discover that she is not appreciated by her patients for trying to be like her analyst.

The flash of a camera broke in on that fantasy. Her patient refused to conform. She was not a "good" patient. Yet she was a good patient—a terrific patient. A very creative person, an insistent person, loyal in her own way. She was not giving up. "I have other voices", said Marge. "It is not only a matter of trying to do good therapy, of being a good analyst. I feel Pam is trying to get through to me, stir me."

"She needs to break the fantasy bubble", I say. "Get to something real."

"But I don't just feel violated as a therapist. I feel violated as a person. *I* feel violated."

Pam *is* getting through, creating a disturbance. It is not simply that Pam is out of control. She spends session time saying what she goes through. She beats against walls trying to take pictures, trying to exhibit, trying to persevere through states of disintegration that paralyse her. She works with and fights the limitations of who she is and what she can do. She presses Marge to do the same.

"I doubt if Pam could stay with a therapist she could not violate", I ventured.

Marge is a searching, creative therapist, afraid, as well as proud, of her own creativeness. She underwent training to get her creativity under control, to harness it in a discipline. Now a patient takes her to the edge of her discipline. What she has learned is not enough to help her in the living present. But her learning is not without value. It gives access to a therapy world and enables her to speak. It has brought her to a place that requires more.

It does not take long to run through a number of permutations in symbolic dance. Marge suspects she tastes violation that pulverized Pam as the latter's personality formed. If she cannot endure a smidgen of what ripped Pam, what sort of therapist is she? Is she not supposed to tolerate what the patient cannot? Marge worked for years understanding and surmounting wounds in her beginnings—violation is no stranger to her. With care, she found ways to build a life that is basically good for her. She lives a comfortable enough existence in which the sense of violation is manageable. Pam certainly is not threatening her whole existence, just part of it. For a time, the sense of lacerating violation mounts, floods the room, but Marge and Pam go home and, one way or another, continue living.

Marge instinctively knows that violation, so alive between them, is a form of communication that ought not be shut down. She knows it is a valuable signifier of wounds and a challenge to growth. Knowledge is one thing, reality is another. It is one thing to know what two-year-olds do, another to face it. It is easy to write a patient (or therapist) off as manipulative and controlling and to battle for boundaries. It is something else to realize that what is at stake is discovery and the creation of what it is possible to experience.

What *is* it possible to experience? Is this not, partly, what therapy is about? If the therapist loses sight of this adventure, a patient may remind her. By the time I saw Marge, she was so stressed by what to do about Pam's behaviour in sessions that she dreaded seeing Pam even more than she dreaded seeing her supervisor. She prayed that the session would be over before it started. She just hoped to get through without disaster. She tried telling and not telling Pam the violation she felt, sharing interpretations, possibilities. Pam might enter the sharing but, in the end, remain impervious—as if she herself came to represent the uninterpretable, the recalcitrant, the ungovernable. Marge almost reached the point where the main thing experienced in therapy was dread of therapy.

I suggested that she shift her focus from Pam's behaviour to what she herself was feeling. No matter what Pam does or does not do, keep feeling what you feel. Pam's behaviour is less important than feelings it generates. Pam's behaviour is a gateway to experiential worlds that are barely opening.

I do not mean that behaviour is unimportant—on the contrary. But the anxiety it initially generates thwarts the development of further experience it might mediate. Marge was stuck in the split between maintaining boundaries and acting impulsively: should I or shouldn't I? What may be more important than action or inaction is connecting with her own experiential field. Perhaps she was stuck in a first, or second, or third "take" on what was happening between her and Pam. Even from her first outpourings to me, so much swirled in her experiencing. What about fidelity to the swirl as such, rather than siding with any part? Maybe making room for the fact of uncertainty in a situation is as important as anything else.

Even a small shift in attitude makes a striking difference:

1. Within a few supervisory sessions, Marge felt less tense and worried. "I felt pressure to know what to do. I couldn't simply be at a loss. It's a relief to think I don't have to 'solve' this. I don't have to know what I *should* do. I can keep not knowing if I really don't know." Not knowing makes room for more experiencing.

2. Lowering the pressure to know enabled Marge to acknowledge her deeper faith—in the face of all fears—that their bond was more durable and precious than anything that happened or failed to happen at any one time. Marge had not fully taken in the fact that Pam was giving her and therapy time to develop. In spite of deeper intimations, Marge succumbed to an anxiety generated by the immediate pull of Pam's actions. She repeatedly—temporarily—broke faith with her most basic conviction that good would come of their contact. She did not have to be a therapy saint. I suspect she sought me out to help her have faith in her faith.

3. Shifting her focus from Pam to herself reminded Marge that therapy is a learning experience, not a finished product. The pressure to take a stand diverted attention from what was most precious in her experience. The pressure to "be" a therapist masked what she knew most of all: two human beings were in a room together, and the experience of both mattered. She was afraid to believe in the place inside where Pam's taking or not taking pictures mattered less than what was ripening below the surface.

4. The sense of violation is an object of mystery and a point of study. It is fathomless. We can point to many apparent causes of violation, some horribly obvious. It is important to do this in order to get a grip on what torments us and assert our right to exist and flourish in face of it. Yet violation outlasts and subtends our list of causes. Freud's "primary repression" is one attempt to reflect on violation as a precondition for the possibility of psychic life as we know it. The fact that we live in an explosive, radioactive black-hole universe suggests that violation may be part of our capacity to experience. In mythology, creativity is often associated with violation. The sense of violation spurs meditation.

The fact that Marge felt personally violated by Pam made violation real, indisputable, raw. Neither could wish it away. Being a "therapist" does not help. Violation can be smelled, tasted—it has to be acknowledged. To the extent that violation can be nibbled at, partly metabolized, understood, turned into stories, works of art, therapy interventions, better personal and socioeconomic situations—all the better. Violation can never be fully metabolized. It is an ever-present fact. Even so, we challenge it. Therapy challenges it. Aspects of religion and politics challenge it. We envision nonviolation, less violation, and we work towards it, even though we are enmeshed in it and challenges to violations result in other violations.

Pam presents violation as a fact in the hope that it will go away—in the hope that Marge can do something about it, perhaps the way a mother soothes a baby. Many people hope that therapy can cure violation. Yet therapy is not violation-free. It can be immensely violating. Do we imagine that therapeutic poisons act as semi-antidote to worse poisons and build immunity? Pam violates Marge as an image of Marge violating Pam. Pam knows how violating therapy is, what a violation just going to therapy can be. Pam also knows that therapy has been good for her—but can something good last? Pam tests the waters to see whether therapy will be worse than what already scars her. She knows that therapy, like everything else, can turn into something horrible.

The truth is that Marge has already passed the test. Pam tests therapy in manageable doses. She does not make therapy totally impossible. Pam tests Marge's convictions, shakes her up. She forces Marge to dig into what she believes. How real is therapeutic faith—what is it able to sustain? What is Marge's vision of therapy? Pam exacts a price. If she grows, Marge grows; if she stretches, Marge stretches. She demands that therapy grow with her—she will not grow alone. The fact that Marge seeks help is testimony to Pam's faith in her. Faith follows violation's trail.

A prosthetic device

"Isn't Pam's camera a kind of prosthetic device?" I asked one day. "A little like an artificial limb. Maybe it helps support a part of her mind."

It seemed to me that Pam's camera might try to make up for a deficit, perhaps be an attempt to see and feel, or gain support for seeing and feeling. In fact, Marge felt this way too, but she had been afraid to trust herself.

There are somewhat harsher possibilities that are equally valid. We are looked at from birth and see ourselves looked at (Paul, 1997): the "seeing eye" is installed in our "mind's eye". We see ourselves seeing and being seen. This sense of an omnipresent eye transforms into the idea that God is always watching us, and the "evil eye" is ever lurking. The sense of an "evil watcher" who persecutes us is a staple of psychosis. The "watcher" can swallow existence. One may so identify with "seeing" that emotional spontaneity, well-toned contact with the flow of body life, and an engaged "feel" for the reality of other people fades or fails to get sufficiently established. Many people who come for help carry a "cruel eye" that threatens to wreck existence.

It may be that the camera objectifies the "seeing eye" and intensifies disembodied seeing. It is a machine, not flesh. It does not feel. It presents profiles, one eye-shot after another. The camera reinforces dehumanized visual dominance and represents rather than heals madness.

More often, a recovering patient shows her pictures with a sense of real pleasure and satisfaction and, more, a touch of awe, astonishment, wonder—as if saying, "God! Look at this! Life! Isn't it amazing?" At the same time that she shares her enchantment with the "object", she shares her growing enjoyment of self: "Look what I did! Look at *my* picture." She shares her engagement with a bit of reality that made her feel more alive, something she has seen and, in addition, something the camera disclosed to her. Her camera supports interpenetration of seeing and feeling in a relatively safe and comfortable way.

My suspicion is that many patients who dream of and/or use a camera as part of a process of recovery suffered serious trauma mixed with moments of exquisite gratification while gazing at a mother's or father's or caretaker's face in infancy. There are moments when a human face is the centre of the cosmos, like the centre of a variegated, undulating, living mandala (Eigen, 1993, pp. 49–104). Golden halos around saints in medieval paintings portray the glow every infant sees.

This glow gets ruptured, soiled, injured. The face one stares at can turn into something horrible, damaging, damaged. There are horror movies that depict such deformations. A beautiful face becomes terrifying or disintegrates before one's eyes. Images, once kept apart in art, are superimposed on each other today. It is not only a matter of ecstasy replaced by dread, although that is genuine enough. It is the very change from one to the other that freezes aspects of the self. There are individuals in a kind of vibrating paralysis, at once overchilled and overheated, alive beyond endurance in mixtures of beauty and ghastliness.

It is as if one's body almost relaxes and surrenders to a taste of something wonderful, but gets pulverized, tenses, and grips itself tightly from within. An inner carapace develops, spreading along muscular, neurological, and circulatory lines. One's psychophysical being congeals, partly, in fright. The fright is packed with fury.

At the same time, images of self and/or other decompose and harden in variable states of decomposition. One exists in degrees of shatter that span somatopsychic realities. With enough therapy, one can slow down the projector and see the transition between the beautiful face and the destroyed one. One can, in imaginative vision, build endurance for looking into fusions of beatific love and sickening destruction. Individuals may be virtually helpless against such fusions yet find ways to hold fast to tiny islands of coherence that form, are lost, then reform.

A camera sometimes provides or expresses moments of coherence. It presents enduring images beyond the shatter. For a time, the images may not include people. The terrors of disintegrating faces are mercifully avoided. One buys time for rehabilitation among the world of objects built by humans, so that one feels humanity through the latter's products, as well as wonders and shocks of nature. A field with a barn and plough in the distance, a flower that opens like face, heart, genitals. Humanity and nature commingle, inform each other. The wounded individual tries to heal.

There are, also, images of devastation, bits of hands, body parts, face with no emotion, terrors that savour hints of bliss. My experience is that as therapy goes on, a poignant sense of time and loss gradually mitigates the blankness. It makes sense that, at some point, some patients will want to focus on the analyst's face. It becomes important whether the analyst's face is part of the blankness or possesses pockets of life a patient may use.

As I looked at Marge, I definitely felt that her face possessed life her patient could use. I felt areas of tightness, anxiety, blank spots, dominance, but, overall, a basically good feeling. She was psychically connected, daring, caring—someone a creative patient at loose ends, living at the edge of nerve shatter, could feel good about. My deepest intimation was that Pam's taking pictures of Marge was a way of letting Marge's good feelings in.

Taking the pictures made Pam feel good. Moreover, she was taking pictures of something in Marge that made her feel good. For the moment, her camera functioned like a baby's mouth—tasting Marge, taking Marge into her, beginning to digest Marge. We only want to put good things into our mouths. More than mouth—eyes, soul windows. Marge was the apple of Pam's eyes. She saw something of the goodness of life in Marge's face. The camera made it safer to connect image with feeling. Taking Marge's picture was a way of affirming the fact of psychic nourishment, a process with many twists and turns.

The camera gave Pam some sense of momentary control over what was inside/outside her. But less important than control was the affirmation that there was something worth breaking rules for, something worth shooting, ingesting, developing. There was something she valued, affirmed, felt strongly about. She herself did not know exactly what she was doing or what was happening, but she valued the special sense within that egged her on.

Sometimes a therapist gets just the patient she needs to enable her to come into her own, to become the therapist she was meant to be. Perhaps Pam was doing this for Marge. The only thing that could ruin their therapy, I thought, was if Marge lost out to her fears and failed to let herself become the therapist she sensed she could be, the therapist Pam was calling her to become.

A few years after our first consultation, Marge brought some pictures Pam was exhibiting. They were marvellous, fresh, Pam's own. They included photos/constructions of Marge in ways that extend the range of experiencing faces. Upon seeing them, I realized that we ever create the human face anew. We portray, repair, and inflict damage, shake bits of reality into configurations through which light shines differently and visual textures create new enchantments. The radiant glow, not lost in spite of the destruction it goes through, surprises one in the turns it takes. With new faces come new bodies; with new bodies—new faces.

CHAPTER SIX

The world gets bigger

"Laura"

"I'm growing in a way that'll enable me to survive being alive", says Laura.

Laura has been working on herself for years. She sees into herself, feels herself, tries to salvage seeds of integrity. She does not give up on herself. She is now in her fifties, and she works harder than ever, sees more, feels more.

She is proof that the dead come alive and seek more and more life. However, a point comes when one does not know what to do with aliveness one discovers.

From the outset, Laura saw herself as growing in inimical circumstances. Her mother was abrasive, critical, rejecting, yet she expected loyalty. Her father was caring and calm but distant, involved in work. He respected Laura's freedom, separateness. She admired his ability to be cool and reflective and felt a quiet core of love—not enough to protect her in a daily way from mother's onslaughts and scorn.

A mother's love mixed with rage seared and scarred her. Laura felt that she grew in a poisonous atmosphere that regularly flared into higher bursts of awfulness. A sense of devastation lodged in her chest. Since Laura pinned feeling crushed to mother's rage and ridicule, she nurtured the belief that one day she would free herself by growing up and leaving home.

One of the amazing things about being a bully parent is the amount of devotion one commands. The temper tantrum tyrant storms the nest the child has in her heart, and the latter's love grows around whatever is there. In Laura's case, child love grew around an exploding bomb, devotion melded around devastation.

"Someday I'll be free", the child promises herself, picturing growing up as freedom. For a while, growing up almost works. The world gets bigger in secondary school, and at university. Still, the devotional tie to a bully parent one wants to break from has repercussions. Laura "solved" the tension between devotion and freedom by marrying her college love.

For some years, she and her husband, "Will", were free together. They worked, explored life, travelled, tasted aliveness. The core of caring in Laura's heart found a place in Will's. As time went on, a bullying tendency in Will grew, or Laura noticed it more.

The constricting force she tried to escape from resurfaced in her marriage.

There were major differences between Will and her family. Will was not rageful like her mother, not blastingly annihilating. But Laura was infuriated by the way he casually assumed that he was right, as if only he existed. He took it for granted that she would fall in with him. It took years for Laura to realize that Will chose where to live, how to arrange their house, where they went on holiday, and most other elements of lifestyle. In the early glow of marriage it felt as if they were sharing life together, and she quieted her doubts. She discovered life in ways Will opened for her. As the years went on, differences grew. The little world they created, largely on his terms, became stultifying. She began reaching beyond it, including finding therapy.

"It's not that Will's a tyrant like my mother. But it's there. He assumes things will be his way, that I'll give in. It's not that he doesn't listen to me. It's worse. He doesn't even know I'm talking. It doesn't dawn on him I might have something valid to say. It's not just getting shut out. The category that I might really *be* there is missing."

It was years before Laura connected with the sense that *she* was missing. Her not being in her own life was something she had wondered about since early childhood, although not in an explicit way. A mute sense of not quite being there was built into how it felt to be alive. She got so used to semi-vanishing in the face of mother's battering and father's absence that she did not even realize that she was not there and continued this with Will. She grew accustomed to living quietly in a numb haze. Yet she was there in her fear, anger, and good moments. She was in her waiting. Laura waited for years to show up more fully, and there is an implicit sense of being in waiting to be.

Her not being there was a temptation for Will to pour himself into space she might have occupied. There is grim, amazing logic in the formation of couples. Will wanted to run things and "chose" a woman not there enough to oppose him. Laura needed to jump-start her life and found in Will a way out of her family, a way into a wider world. She needed his self-assertion to catapult her to another phase of living. For a time, being "bullied" expanded her life.

Laura recognized in Will's self-assertion a missing part of herself. She did not want to assert herself so blindly and simply as Will. But she needed in her way what he held for her.

Little did she suspect he would be a training ground for her self-assertion. She pitted herself against him by degrees. He tried intimidating her with anger, arguments, and disdain, but she gathered her forces and persevered. He tried flicking her off with male superiority, egocentric confidence. Battles went on for years, never-ending. Nothing stopped her for long.

Why did they stay together? Laura's first therapist encouraged her self-awareness and fortified her for the fight. He did not think the marriage would last—or *should* last. A college marriage to escape home—how could it last? Neither Laura nor Will had the personality to support a marriage. Neither had a clue to what marriage was about.

They were too immature to marry.

Egged on by therapy, Laura left Will several times. Her marriage reformed, and she left therapy instead. Laura felt that her first therapy was important. It got her started. But she did not like getting pushed into making a move she might regret for the rest of her life. It was easy for the therapist to talk about finding herself. He did not have to live with her or live her life. Perhaps he was better equipped to do what he advised. He was, after all, on his third marriage. What worked for him might not work for her. His words were not enough to get her through. No one would be with her in moments of truth, through painful nights and agitated days. She was unwilling to give Will up to grow in imaginary ways.

Laura's second therapy continued to strengthen her. She read enormously and began to see pervasive power struggles in human interactions. A predatory drive for dominance permeated her life. Her mother and father fought for supremacy in different ways: rage versus remoteness, reactivity versus reflection. Subgroups in the workplace competed to be on top. People talked about democracy but grabbed at power. Words were forming for what she felt all her life. Tensions that had ripped and crushed her as a child began to find a conceptual frame of reference.

Her marriage was no different from the body politic or her family. Who was on top, who was on the bottom—she or Will? Always a hierarchy. How do emotional and material spoils get divided at any moment? Where does mutuality come in?

Struggle everywhere, more than she bargained for. The possibility of sanctuary disappeared, and Laura became depressed. Anxiety reached a high point, turned off, and depression took its place. She remained prone to agitated depression for many years. There were periods she could not go to work. Her second therapist prescribed medication, and that brought some relief.

When I saw Laura, she was torn between the need to stop the medication in order to feel herself more fully and the need to stay on it in order to function. She felt stuck in her therapy and was afraid to leave it. She began finding excuses to see her therapist less often and eventually tested me out. Laura was angry at her therapist for intensifying her conflict with everyone and everything. She became hopelessly infuriated with the way he stood above the storm, smugly right about everything, imperturbably dominant. He was worse than her husband. His impatience with her marriage intensified her frustration. When his marriage broke up, his disparagement of hers increased.

Laura did not end her marriage but agitated for long-range change. Life inside the bond may be constricting, but she did not trust that there would be much for her outside the bond either. Her bond with Will was unsatisfactory but real. Her intuition said that she was unlikely to find anything as real again. Her path was to make her situation better, not to jettison it.

When I saw her, she was an agitated ball of conflict whirring in circles trying to move on. Without medication, she would not have been able to move at all. With medication, she felt silly, frivolous, forgetful. Fury grew. Medication helped her to sleep and somewhat calmed her during the days. Yet discomfort never left her: "I am nervous, always nervous. Medication makes me feel as if I'm not nervous, but I *am*. What worries me is that the meds are affecting my brain. I can't remember things at work. I end up looking silly, like I don't know what I'm doing. I blurt things out, but I'm not sure what I say is what I want to say.

"Of course the meds affect my brain. That's what they're supposed to do. What I'm afraid of is that they're permanently affecting it, causing permanent damage, that I'll never be able to get my memory back, even if I get off them. I feel watery. What I say runs off the top, lacks substance. It's hard for me to stay in contact at a level that lets me feel I'm me. I spill about. My therapist doesn't like it when I tell him I cut down the meds."

For the first several years of our work, Laura failed in attempts to wean herself from medication. If she cut down, she could not sleep and was angry, tired, or paranoid at work. Within a week or two she would become depressed and agitated. She went back and forth, trying to find a way to balance the need to function and feel like herself.

She told me all the things she did not like about her previous therapists, her husband, her family, work, our world. Would someone be hearing similar things about me someday?

She told me all the things she liked too. She was very good at her work and had nourishing interests. Both therapists had helped her in important ways, and her marriage, whatever its ills, was strong (even when shaky). Over the years, Will began to listen to Laura, through her effort. He wanted to grow as well, to some extent. He remained basically himself, but he became a little more open to what she needed. Sometimes she got through, often not. But the opening grew, and things were not completely static.

Her past therapists had left their marriages to seek a better life. Who knows the future, but so far I have stuck with mine. I know well how it feels to suffer daily traumas in a close relationship, and I can empathize with Laura's willingness to stick it out. I am patient with her distress and the insolubility of daily issues. I have lived with insoluble difficulties all my life. I suspect that one difference between myself and Laura's earlier therapists is that I am not proactive when it comes to difficult problems. I often do not know which way to go and can wait for a long time for things to evolve.

Some patients leave marriages, some stay in them. I could imagine I play a role in which way they go, but years of work suggest that an outcome has a life of its own, that I am more like a Greek chorus, echoing, emphasizing, responding to obscure forces playing themselves out. Now I am entering old age and feel life stirring in me somewhat differently. I may be tougher, but my heart opens more easily. It does not take much for the smile at the core of my heart to spread. I can sit for hours and listen appreciatively to Laura's difficulties. So much colour, music, brokenness. I like listening. I feel I hear life speaking. I learn about everything by feeling another person's struggles.

I hear good things, bad things, the depression Laura cannot beat, anxiety that will not go away, fruitless struggles of one against all, moments of awakening, bursts of vision, creative strivings endangered by destructive realities. In my old age, not knowing what to do has become an art form. I feel more and more liberated from the need to correct or reform or hunt "pathology" (life itself may be pathological). The need to act diminishes while reflective appreciation, mixed with awe and wonder, grows.

It is not doing nothing that is therapeutic, but the way one does nothing. Laura was never in a situation in which she felt so little pressure from another person: no one telling her what to do, no one *knowing* what to do, someone who just liked being in a room with her, hanging out in a therapeutic kind of way. It gave her time to hear herself, to go over her life, her daily trials, defeats, hopes, impossibilities—the wretchedness of our world and its glorious promises.

As the years unfolded, she felt that she was doing all she could to be herself. She began to appreciate her struggle against negative forces inside and outside herself. She felt better about her try at living. She was glad that she stayed with Will. Their relationship provided backbone, stability, richness over decades. Yes, their relationship was stultifying, but without it life would have been bleaker.

Deep down, she knew she would not leave Will and that she had best make the most of what they could have together. This meant, too, making the most of what she could do on her own. She never stopped finding ways to make things better. She would extend edges, discover lines between barriers, come upon surprising openings. The model was not the dissolution of barriers so much as loving the flowers growing within the walls.

After a decade, Laura began talking about leaving me. She wondered whether our therapy had reached a point of diminishing returns. I do not know whether or not she will leave or when, but I am delighted that she is talking about it. She never talked through leaving with a therapist before. Do I know whether she *should* stay or go? Not in the least. She is welcome to stay as long as she likes or leave whenever she wants to. I am delighted she saw me as long as she did, I delight in her person, being, and energy. Something happened in our work, although I cannot say what or how.

She speaks of miracles. She cannot believe that she has been medication-free almost a year, finds ways of sleeping through nights, feels better during days. The people at work no longer personify evil but are, like herself, afflicted with grave difficulties. There is evil in life, society, self—and a great majority of us, stupid and blind, are brothers and sisters in profound struggle against great odds. If we are enemies of one another, we are also friends. Laura feels this kinship, this potential partnership. I think it one of life's most precious hopes.

Laura feels a bond with other people as flawed as she. It is a bond she nurtured all her adult life with Will—a flawed bond, a bond of life. Now it extends, in variable degrees, to others. No one was more surprised than Laura to feel growth of tolerance—even appreciation—of people she had once mistrusted. Capacity for mutual injury and hate remained. Awareness of complexity of factors that make up experience grew. Perception of evil was no less intense. But the boundary between Laura and the Enemy shifted. She could feel more people from the inside and not simply place them on the other side of the line. Laura found a place where damaged bonds unite us.

What was Laura's depression about? Was it biochemical?—a result of emotional injury?—a combination of physical and social factors? Chemical treatment seemed necessary for a time and helped up to a point. But Laura wanted something more. She could not reconcile herself to the veil that medication placed between her and her experience. I never suggested that she should come off medication, and I did not stop her from experimenting. I felt the pain of her quandary and was as perplexed as she. I could only be with her in her attempt to find a way to be with herself.

In time, I began to feel that Laura was in a crisis of faith. She stumbled onto the predatory vision of life—survival of the powerful. I cannot say what "fittest" might mean, but I do not necessarily equate fit with powerful. Faith asks whether there is a fit between ourselves and our world, our universe, our God, ourselves, yet is capable of surviving and being enriched by a good deal of lack of fit. At times, power has the painful yet positive function of destroying rigid fits, creating destructive imbalances, generating new possibilities. It is not a simple matter of faith versus power. There are people, indeed, who have faith, so to speak, only in power. Laura's crisis touches the question of what makes being alive worth while, what sort of person ought one to be, what sort of being can one say "yes" to? She was appalled to see how much life hung on power. Does might make right? Is there room for love, or is love child's play, wish-fulfilment, a side-show? What is central, what is peripheral?/are contraries impossibly mixed?

It was not simply that Laura was one of the weak. She did not *want* to be one of the powerful, subjugating others. She hoped that life could be more than this. She knew the pain of being one of the weak, and she did not merely want to turn the tables. A hidden question she brought to therapy was: is it a human possibility to be in a room with another person and not have to fight and fight and fight? I do not know if this is a resolvable issue, or whether we can be alone without fighting ourselves. Perhaps there are different ways of fighting, some more productive than others. Perhaps observing the Sabbath means that there is a point in the soul where peace reigns. It is a question to ask and think about. Laura wanted something more than her world seemed to offer, perhaps more than life *can* offer. What faith in life is possible if life is the villain?

A crisis of faith was precipitated by the intimation that the Enemy was inherent in life itself.

Most of us are no match for the Enemy in direct combat (for a description of one man's successful fight with an inner dream enemy, see Eigen, 1995.) The sense of pervasive evil in life brought Laura low. Therapy provided a place to voice indignation, to protest, to document injustice, and to go on saying whatever she saw. She could let her truth unfold without someone silencing her, without someone trying to convince her that it was not so or that it had to be this way. Therapy gave Laura a taste of what communication (communion) within wider personal boundaries can do.

If we ceaselessly struggle for dominance, we can, nonetheless, create different ways of relating to that fact. We can oppose our oppositional nature and channel it. We can situate diverse tendencies within a broader field of vision that leaves room for opposition. We can turn oppositions into questions. One of the precious things about faith is that it can question everything. Not to do so is constricting. Laura questioned *everything* in her life and world. An incessantly tested sense of goodness survived the onslaught. Embattled goodness may be fragile and tenuous, ever torn apart, renewable—the farther we go, the deeper the glow.

Sometimes I felt as if an angel helped to plug Laura into another being whose damage worked with hers. Resources buried in the ability to cling to an aching bond helped to see her through. Damage in the heart of the good can stimulate growth of compassion in face of despair. Laura held on to therapy long enough for such a turn to take hold.

"Milton"

Milton sees evil everywhere, especially in himself. He relentlessly perceives evil in human motivation. He was not always this way. He remembers loving his father with all his heart. As a little boy, he trusted and admired his father with all his being. He has access to these feelings only as a memory that rubs salt in wounds. Any rise of love feeds an abiding sense of injustice.

Yet Milton's wife opens her heart to him. Whatever injury, her heart keeps opening. His children open their hearts too. No matter what they go through, their hearts keep opening. Milton lives amidst love, a world of love, but he cannot feel it without nullifying it. Love is real, but inside himself it sours.

You would think that love around him would signify love within him. Milton can think this as an idea, but it has no living meaning. He cannot feel it in a way that counts, in a way that stays, in a way that survives his constant assaults. He is an appealing man who tries to be the caring person he cannot feel himself to be. He tries his best in life, he gives everything he can. But there is some way he cannot *feel* this giving. He stays in therapy because he discounts *everything* that others find positive in him. In fact—and so far I have failed to convey the heart-wrenching, bloodcurdling nature of his plight—the only thing that he feels is real and true is his ability to attack whatever might be real and true. The deep truth of his being is that only an annihilating force is real. Nothing else in himself *feels* believable.

His wife's and my heartfelt anguish bear the gap between love and the force ever annihilating it. *We* feel the realness of love devoured by hate and injury. Perhaps Milton is grateful we are there to hold what he cannot bear, the love he x's out. But that is not the point, as he tells me over and over. The point is that love gets x'd out, and only destruction of it feels real. If that is not grasped, all the love in the world is beside the point. If the realness of destruction going on in the core of his being is not recognized, love is valueless, gratitude is irrelevant.

Milton's wife tries to convince him that there is something good in him. She is extremely resourceful. She never gives up. Recently she launched a new attack on his addiction to his annihilating disposition: "You are your father, after all. Instead of pleasure, you are preoccupied with dysphoria. Your father's self-importance is transmitted through your obsessive self-dysphoria. You make yourself the centre of attention with it. You talk about it all the time."

Those are fighting, cutting words; truthful, compassionate words. Milton's self-preoccupation posits him as the effective centre of life, an impotent centre. Yet what power impotence wields! It pulls everything towards it. It leaves no room for anything else.

Milton's self-horror deepens as he stares into the mirror his wife holds up to him. His father saved him from his mother, a drug addict who was out of it much of the time. Milton lived in chaos. He longed for his father to come and rescue him. His father's intermittent visits whet his longing. At last—too late, Milton now feels—his father gained parental rights and took him away. Another hell began.

Hell came by degrees. Milton did not know what had hit him. At first, heaven: life away from mother. His father got out of bed in the morning, worked, had women—a very active man, very into life's chores and pleasures. He became the centre of Milton's life . . . a centre that often was not there.

His father was filled with a sense of self-importance: his father, the messiah. To Milton he seemed bigger than life. He loved to be admired and found people who looked up to him. Milton was one of a crowd of admirers. Milton's pain grew as his father's ego displaced his own, as he became a satellite moon around Father Jupiter.

In therapy, Milton never ceased being a spokesperson for respect. If there was one ingredient fatally missing from his early life, that was respect: respect for the sacred being of another—neither his father nor mother had a glimmer of it. Each was self-absorbed in her or his way. His father's need to be worshipped precluded his ability to see the other as a centre of being in a full-bodied way. His mother, on the other hand, was a collapsed star, moments of shining beauty embedded in infinite morass.

Worshipful love turned to agonized rage. There comes a time when pressure to be oneself rips through attempts to fit another's desire. Milton's eyes and heart grew cold as he distanced himself from his father. More than anything, he did not want to be someone enamoured by self-importance. He did not want to be a psychological predator needing others as ego food. Normal ways that people use each other to enhance self-esteem became abhorrent. Milton became a critic of the human condition, scenting deficiencies and lies in everything a person did. Most of all, rage hardened into abiding self-hatred. There was nothing he could do that passed his eye's test. He lacerated himself for any trace of self-importance or wish for love. Everything masked a corrosive core.

There was nothing to support his fight with his father. When he began pushing away, he fell into a hole. Beneath his father was his collapsed mother. Inner support was missing. There were moments his mother was alive and beautiful and moments when he could be proud of his father's show of confidence. But he looked on in horror as his mother disintegrated. He tightened as he watched his father try to con the world and put one over on life.

Inwardly, he fought double annihilation—being sucked into father's shining ego and mother's morass. Pain grew, coupled with a sense of injustice and rage. Hate cemented his personality and became a kind of cobalt cover, as envisioned by General MacArthur, sealing a boundary.[1] Lost inside the cobalt cover was burnt, trembling fear. An annihilating core took the place where a mother and father might have been. In one or another form, Milton was what he fought.

At the same time, Milton learned enough from his father to appear confident in the world. On the outside, he seemed to have his act together. The very fact that he was proud of his good appearance increased his self-mistrust. He hated himself the more for being able to pull off the illusion of a good life, although his self-contempt would be even greater if he failed.

One day he remarked that he stayed at the edges of his personality and the periphery of life, because "going to the centre is too terrifying". The deeper he goes, the greater the annihilating force. He fears that nothing can withstand it. It is better to stay on the edge of hate, to be condescending and sarcastic, than be consumed. It is safer to be on the border of fear than to burn in its centre. Thus Milton gives deeper meaning to the mixture of pride and self-contempt he feels in being a "cool" person.

He begins his journey towards the centre by degrees—degrees of hell: "There are moments my wife or children touch me and I feel as if I can be touched on the inside of my body. My body softens, and I cringe with fear. A second wave of fear turns into terror, void, emptiness, cold space. Maybe if I could tolerate being

---

[1] In the 1950s, after the U.S. Army was routed by the Chinese, General Douglas MacArthur put forward a plan to sow a belt of radioactive cobalt to create a permanent radioactive barrier between North and South Korea.

touched on the inside of my body, coldness would be more tolerable. Coldness: my royal position, my king space.

"People are peacocks. They flex their feathers to be seen and
selected, the superior ones. That's all that activates them. It's a clear
experience inside my body. No matter how much you sympathize,
care, love me, there'll always be the moment that turns. You'll
vitiate the meaning of what I am saying. You'll try to put me in my
place or lose connection and just speak out. You'll be filled with
yourself and lose contact with me.

"It's possible to tell by the inside of one's body whether another
person has done that or whether they stay in contact and mean
what they say. I *know* you are fallible, and I *ought* to cut you slack.
I am blocked off from the very thing I crave and recognize. I am
compelled to feel what you give and who you are as inauthentic,
reckless, an appearance, as it is in me. I'll box in and prevent the
return of the sensation, shut off the appeal of being touched."

At moments, Milton feels the cold void as self-protective, secondary. But when he dips into it, it becomes overwhelming and
primary. It instantaneously eats all warmth. He points to my failures and concludes that I am like all the others, including himself—
a vain peacock or incapable of sustaining or believing in contact.
There is no room for love, only for vanity and incapacity, if not
outright meanness. All grace is pretence—except that he sees it
shining in his wife's heart and in the face and touch of his children.
He turns to ice and becomes an empty crater when he begins to feel
them inside his body.

After much work, Milton confesses to glimpsing specks of
goodness buried deep within: "The disease process got to a lot of
tissue, but not all." "I feel something [good] buried. I feel as if I
could bring it to the surface through active dead zones."

As soon as these words escape his lips, destruction accelerates:
"I was a good boy. Good like Jesus. Feeling superior in phoney
goodness to make up for real badness. If I idealize others, they'll
listen to me. Jesus getting killed on behalf of Father's limitless
narcissism. I could be a special person by being good and getting
killed."

The rise of goodness is squelched instantaneously, reinter-
preted as seductive, manipulative, escapist. From there, the slide
continues.

"You're thinking: 'If you just didn't x out the loving feelings—
if you just didn't attack them. *You're* doing this to yourself.' You
think it's something I do to myself, something I can control, something I ought to be able to stop or redirect."

I am thinking nothing of the sort. But I know I am the stand-
in for well-wishers and do gooders and voluntarists who try to
convince him he *can* contact the good in himself and live it. I am
also the proxy for people who love him. I am not sure what I am
feeling exactly, but I am in the throes of watching destruction at
work, as if allowed a privileged view of self-annihilation in process.
Milton is used to being blamed for his blackness. His father thinks
Milton is emotionally self-indulgent. He should snap out of it, get
on with it.

"I can't find anything else. Maybe there *is* nothing else except
malevolence at this level."

I feel the cut of his pain, his agony. It is pure hell in the place he
lives. I am prepared to be in hell for ever. While awake, there is a
way I begin to black out and lose consciousness in the pain. I am
amazed to hear him speak of a gold bar.

"There's a gold bar in some place in the middle of the deadness.
Is it for real? There's something that's not contaminated? I see it
but can't access it, and it's not there all the time. Malevolence is
there all the time. Images of a guy coming through the door and
feeling I'm going to be raped. I'm always feeling I'm about to be
raped. There's something in my eyes that cuts through everything,
and I want to evacuate it. I want to evacuate my body. Is something
else there? Really? Or is even the softening a lie, a way of appearing
to myself and others as something other than malevolent, an amel-
iorating, appealing softness, a protection?

"The five-year-old was not filled with this darkness. I was
wide-eyed, stunned, freaked out at the violence between my parents. I turned serpentine, malicious. These two states of being are
split. Innocent, loving kid—I don't want him back. Hate waves are
too deep to mobilize any effective reaction against them. Is there an
alternative to killing myself? Can it be I've come to hate two child
versions of myself and that I'll never be able to embrace them? The
loving child, the hating child—stupid submitting fools. I won't be a
fool now. I don't want father's contempt. I'll fight to the end
against submitting and being another foolish child."

To hate his father and mother, to hate injustice, violence, injury—is to be a longing soul. Milton is speaking of a time when hate was tied to love, before the love/hate connection soured. This is hot hate. In time, it congealed into serpentine malevolence, detached from love, shooting down any surge of love within. Milton's foolish hate is hopeful hate, when a child's hate hopes to burn a pathway to the parent's heart. Milton refuses with all his might to be a fool again, yet he has not entirely given up on fool's hope. It is a hope he cannot acknowledge and still be true to himself. It is a hope I dare not play on or I will be felt to be an impotent seducer, another well-meaning impostor.

"It is like heaven when I can finally let down. Terrified. Every interaction can be a painful assault, rage, broken, tormented. Heart is stopped. Don't know what to do about my hateful, superior arrogance. I'm a monster and he [father] is a monster. Don't say we all have our dark side. What I need is someone to say, 'I see you don't have a place in you where you feel loving kindness and compassion for others or yourself. It's a *real* problem. I don't have the solution or know if there is one. This doesn't mean there isn't one.' Otherwise, I'm not met. I'm told I have to put on that nice face or you can only see my negativity if it's tempered by 'goodness' underneath. My only hope is for someone to see this, if that is a hope. I will never feel contained enough without someone seeing this.

"It *is* relieving to talk about it. But I'm worried I'm not in it then, just making it feel better. I hate with such vehemence. Below-the-belt level. Penetrating, tearing at places of pleasure. A hateful ripping that eliminates my basic connection to the ground."

Milton depicts a disillusionment process that has gone horribly wrong. He remembers the loving child in ecstatic union with father, on whom he pinned messianic hopes. He sees a loving child in his mind's eye, and the memory tears him apart and his heart freezes. His father played on Milton's messianic hopes in ways that maximized the crash. No mother was there to cushion the fall, and father tended to rub the realization in: "Well, what did you expect? This is the way life is. Don't you think I'm great anyway?"

And yet a gold bar appeared. Was it cold? Neither warm, nor cold—outside opposites? Just the radiance of Self? Once Milton felt that the gold bar was in and across his chest. Perhaps barring feelings? Containing and condensing them? It is my belief that the gold bar is incorruptible, as Milton said. Ever radiant, never dying. Do I believe my belief? What the gold bar is and whether anything can be forever is something I really do not know. Common sense tells me that everything passes. So must the gold bar. A gold bar would also be a heavy thing to carry. Nevertheless, the feeling is akin to Keats's "A thing of beauty is a joy for ever", or William Blake's insistence that all states (mental, imaginative, spiritual) are eternal. Such forever moments give life a fullness of heart, a radiance of being that might as well be eternal—it almost does not matter, if they are not.

Will Milton ever feel the gold of his bar? What good is the radiant Self to him if he cannot be it, live it? Is he living it anyway? The fact that he might be does make a difference, even though the real-life Milton with real-life feelings finds all that is good in him out of reach. And he needs me to vouch for his difficulty, the impossibility of his being.

CHAPTER SEVEN

Filing insides

"Milton"

"I'm critical, bitter, like having a file inside. Not just a file to store bitter memories. A metal file that gnaws experience down to the worst part, and this thing inside points to it and says, 'You see—that's all there is. Just garbage. Just poison. Just evil.'

"My father talked a good game. He had an idealized vision of someplace where people can be their true selves, a heaven on earth. He tried to make me believe in it, and for a time I did. The way life *could* be *if.* The place the *good* people were. By good he meant honest—the truth-seekers. The truth-tellers. That was the thing. You saw the Truth, capital T. You told others truths they didn't want to hear. You were better, a truth-bearer, and that's what really counted.

"What he didn't tell me—and couldn't admit—was the importance of seeing pain on a person's face when you struck. Truth shocks. It brings a look of disbelief, helplessness, hurt. Truth creates a tear, a rent in the garment. And you feel juicy, on top, fulfilled. You are the truth man, and others can't take it. Truth bullets, truth bombs. Truth orgasms. Is there any greater satisfaction? You are helping people be their true selves. You are helping them get to earthly heaven.

"What *did* go along with his heavenly vision, his hope for humanity, was his mistrust of *everyone*. That was the underside that got into me, the critical, bitter part that files everything down. His truth beam, his lie-seeking missile, sought whatever was evil, unethical, everyone's bad spot.

"I can understand the old preachers who saw fire and brimstone and went right for the jugular, the evil vein. Father didn't believe you can correct the defect by understanding it. You have to take hammer and tongs. Now I hammer at everyone, most of all myself, and the defect grows. It doesn't shrink. The more I hammer, the worse it gets. Understanding doesn't work. Hammering doesn't work. Hammering excites pain, sticks tongs into wounds.

"There was a time he made me feel he knew everything. We were partners in laying bare defects. We were creating heaven together. Now I'm stuck in it and can't stop. I see it and won't let it be my whole life. I act outside it and conduct my life as if this weren't inside. I treat others respectfully. I function well. People think I care. But inside I can't break away from him, and even if I died I would feel this destructive hate and fear. Inside me he still knows everything, and the hate never stops. Will there ever be any goodness inside me? Is there any? Can I find it if there is—without vitiating my story? My truth is hate. If I love, will I be a liar? What would real love be like, if there is such a thing?

"I need somebody to surrender to. I don't really believe in God as a sentient entity. But the universe—yes, the universe is part of me, and I'm part of it. But when I feel that, some part of me rears up in arrogance, and I fight and don't have to surrender. It says to the universe: 'I don't have to surrender to YOU.' Like my father who couldn't give himself over and admit that nature is bigger.

"I want to throw up. I've felt nauseous since childhood. It all passes through my body. I want to throw myself up, throw my father up. I want to throw up the hate. If only one could get rid of evil by throwing up. Nothing ever welcomes me with loving arms. I tell myself that if I felt welcome, I could get better. But I know this is not true. Many welcome me. My wife welcomes me. My friends do, my children do. Sometimes I even feel *you* do. Your being with me through this, something is happening, I am changing, your presence makes a difference. But I can't or won't believe it. I know it is so but can't believe it.

"I want to destroy it. The destructive voice says, you're just holding on to your negativity and won't let go—it's *your* fault. The destructive voice aims at me. An evil truth voice not letting up. It's not true, it *seems* true. I'm at a wall. I'm stuck with the accusation that I exist to destroy the loving truth. I exist to affirm my victimization: *you* did this to me. I wish I could piss this all out, but it won't go out, the stream goes in instead."

My patient, Milton, sees immense personality damage, which he relates to a damaging bond with his father. His father crystallized extreme attitudes, splitting the truth-telling function. We need truth to grow, to be real. But truth can be used destructively. We love truth. But truth can be used hatefully. His father used truth to magnify himself at others' expense and to annex others. Truth becomes a poisonous lie. Milton feels endlessly victimized. He blames his father. His father blames others. Blame is passed from generation to generation. A sense of defectiveness permeates humanity from time immemorial, and Milton and his father mediate defect.

Milton's father was going to mend humanity. Instead, he exacerbated wounds. Milton is stuck at an eternal wall. Only destructiveness and victimization feel real. Yet creativity, love, caring are real too. Something in therapy is real. Destructiveness feels more real. Truth is split between destructiveness and affirmation. Both very real.

Part of what therapy does is to persist, endure, outlast destructiveness. But there is destructiveness in therapy too. What can it mean for therapy to outlast itself? To destroy itself? To try again and keep trying again? And this trying—does it eventually seep into the damaged bond and make a difference? Waiting, trying, deep beauty in patience.

"Neil"

Neil comes in and says: "I feel better—a real shift. But why? How? I have the same gripes but feel better." We have been working for a year, three times a week. He has been blaming his wife and kids for being failed versions of themselves, not what he had imagined or hoped for.

He feels especially tricked by his wife. He was struck by her beauty and promise. She responded so completely when they met. Her beauty still strikes him to the quick. She turned off as their relationship grew. "I've always had this problem", she revealed. "I'm excited only when I'm not involved emotionally. The problem is I love you. I'm committed to you, our marriage, our family. That's why I can't feel sexually."

So far, their marriage survives their affairs. When I met Neil, he was still struggling from his most recent affair—a relationship just on the brink of giving him the fulfilment he had always longed for. His partner was intense, totally in the moment. His passionate dreams were coming true. But she kept criticizing him, putting him down. She gave herself in the moment, yet distanced herself as well. How was this possible: deep self-giving coupled with cold distancing? Neil was frustrated.

In our first months of work, I listened to the virtues and lacks of his women. He seemed to feel that his happiness depended on one of them getting better. They came so close to giving him . . . everything—but always there was a breakdown, a flaw, a problem. His women fed him on/off extremes of experience, in which he felt caught between intensity and vacuum. Once I mused: "I wish I could make them better for you. But they're not my patients. You are." At first he felt that I missed the point and underestimated him. I was cutting and deficient (like his women), yet somehow re-centring. I did not want him to leave himself out of his analysis, nor look for life only through his women.

For a time he dodged entry to himself by blaming choices: "What is wrong with me that I choose the women I do?" Neil seemed comfortable with voluntaristic language, as if he should be in control, make better choices. This "wilful" way of speaking chills me: captain of the ship, be on top. Maybe he is right. Control, choice is the way to go. Popular books say so. But it is not my way, not my *Tao*. Why did he choose me? Another bad choice?

Well, all these "choices" are very mixed and mixed up, aren't they?

And his children? He could never have invented them or thought or imagined them, if it had been up to him. They surpass imagining. Such flaws—nothing he would have ordered. Yet his children touch him beyond conception. They make life worth while. They give life a glow. He looks at them and sees God, whether or not he believes. He believes them—their realness.

As he ponders the defective nature of bonds, he begins to fear his love is scarred too. He would die rather than injure his children, but what if he is injuring them unawares? His love of his children brings him to a place beyond will, where life is supported, nourished, annihilated by who one is and isn't: "I can't bear the thought of compounding my kids' problems by being the person I am."

* * *

Neil reports a miracle of light. His wife, "Brenda", makes fun of him, criticizes him, and it does not get him down. He sees himself through her eyes, and something inside laughs. For a split second, he is liberated from himself. Before, he would have become sullen, accusatory. To be put down and not be nasty or blue and go on being OK—this is different. He hears a good kind of inside-himself laughter never heard before, bubbly in a place that once meant fight to the death. Something in therapy is starting to get through to him.

* * *

To put down and be put down seems beginningless. Neil never saw himself as the sort of person who put others down. He has an ideology of respect and caring. He loves life and loves to learn about it. He delights in his perceptions, the impact of things and deciphering them. His lover's stream of accusations made him aware of the put-down aspect of self. He had never been put down so much, not that he remembered. She called him a monster and made him feel that his wish to be with her was poisonous. The very person who provided passionate moments attacked cherished beliefs about himself. She made him feel awful for feeling good.

It did not occur to Neil that he had his own version of a problem his wife faced. Instead of turning off when feeling a bond (as she did), he was turned on more than ever with a lover who put him down. He could not believe that hate excited him. He felt normal, idealized. He repeatedly told me that he had had a relatively normal upbringing and was not as badly off as his lover, wife, children, many he met—and I, I might add. He was not as badly off as his parents, who had sacrificed their lives for their children and hid from themselves. Now hate singed, repulsed and excited him, and he had to admit he was not exempt. Neil glimpsed the Eternal Put-down, a ubiquitous vein of hate, appalled he might be a carrier too. He saw it in others more than in himself and fairly imagined that what applied to others might apply to him. He felt a compelling fascination with how hate works.

* * *

One day, when Neil was talking about the impact of others on his colourful sensitivity, a question swept me: how is it that he can be so affected by others yet so go his own way, as if the impact did not change anything deep down. His emotional lover, who remained coldly detached—did anything change her as feelings raced? His emotions did not accelerate like hers, but the sense of not being changed by what intensely affects him—does he not share this with her in some way?

I think having children changed him—opened channels of love, meaning, injury. But he finds ways around it. *They*—wife, children, lover—stir negatives that take away from his joy of living. If *they* were different, he would suffer fewer impediments to his innate joyousness. *He* is the joy centre, *they* the detractors. This stance persistently reforms, no matter what he goes through. One session he gets to deep feeling, new insight; the next session—*they*. It's like a girdle, a cocoon, a cement casing around or at the core of self, a mental stance that remains impervious and unbudgeable. The heaven within (real, imaginary) is incessantly stifled or tripped up by real people.

I begin to say, one or another way: "How is it you have this wonderful sensitivity, strong life affirmation—yet deep down are unaffected by what you process so well? I picture your sensitivity as a thin mail armouring, vibrating like a tuning fork, yet whatever is doing the vibrating remains out of play. Am I right? Is this so? How can someone so affected by life be so immune?"

"Growing up, I felt I had a secret", Neil says. "I felt less than I should be. Others were brighter, doing better. Then the brightest left to go to other schools, and I went to the top. By default, I became the very highest: number one. Everyone treated me as if I were so smart, after the best left. My relative rank changed. Inwardly I felt I'm not that smart. It was a horrible secret. Years passed with the institutionalizing of me on top. I felt like a fraud, always.

"The same with sports. I shone early, matured early. I knew that when the rest of the boys caught up with me, things would change. For a time the coach talked Olympics, but I knew better. I was no Olympian. Later I was vindicated, my reality sense intact. The terrible secret finally out: I knew all along: I'm not an Olympian, just a good athlete. Thank God there were people who appreciated me realistically."

Part of Neil's struggle is a battle for his reality sense—precious, fragile, durable.

In the realm of mind—in Neil's case being clever at school—the problem is more difficult. In the realm of body—Neil's early athletic ability—image is checked more easily. As others grow, cards reshuffle naturally.

In mental life the agony is prolonged. After higher education, mental buzz continues: I'm a fraud. I do well. Very well. I'm not the best. I'm the best. I'm the worst. What in-between do I belong to? It's hard to find my level. Friction between image and image, and image and events throw one off. A prize-fighter may learn something about place by getting knocked out. Neither flunking out of school nor being valedictorian silences questions about one's place in the mental universe. Neil comes for help because he is knotted up in a space that is too vast and indefinite.

* * *

Early in marriage, Neil pictured himself as a good man, a good husband. He would make his wife happy or at least contribute towards her happiness. He and she would mediate basic goodness for each other. He was caring, kind, thoughtful, passionate. He liked finding ways to lift their day. However, as things unfolded, hopes that being a good husband would win the day were dashed.

Neil overlooked the control factor fused with goodness and was not ready for the pain that comes when goodness fails to bring results. "It was crushing to find that being a good husband didn't work. I still can't believe there is something wrong with my picture of marriage." Two giving people, caring for each other, enhancing each other's existence—finally, a place to truly be oneself with another person and live a full life.

What Neil did not bargain for was the actuality. Brenda did not spend the time he did trying to make their day beautiful. She took things as they came—chores, getting through, spacing out, doing what needed doing, forgetting things. She was too oblivious for his taste. Something similar happened with his lover. She was more absorbed in her reality than in his or theirs. He repeated incredulously that he and his women were not on the same page. They had a different sense of reality. Where was the shared reality?

Neil concluded that the women he committed himself to were more damaged than he. His wife suffered through wrenching family upheavals, moving around a lot, ghastly violence, loss of loved ones. His girlfriend had been abused and neglected, subject to extremes of gratification and deprivation. His own childhood seemed relatively tame—a stable family, no abuse, no radical extremes, a lot of steadiness. Was he trying to find missing intensity through his women? Was he trying to find the damaged self through them?

Neil claimed that he had strong feelings and was fully alive. The hole was that he had no one to share his aliveness with. Why would women not share the fullness of being with him?

His father had been a hard worker, his mother a shadowy figure in the house, an undeveloped personality. They saw to their tasks. Neil felt a goodness but emptiness in their life. He wanted and got more, but fulfilment eluded him because of a failure in sharing. In the end, his partners withheld themselves or were unable to match his giving. In some crucial way, in spite of all his plenitude, life fed him holes. Still, Neil never gave up on plenitude.

How could there be such a gap between his own and another's reality, particularly that of someone close to him? For Neil, the very closeness of the other made the gap more painful. The difference he expected would become a source of joy turned out to be devastating.

"Life plays with your sense of reality", I say. "So near—so far. You almost get it, but it manages to be somewhere else or not at all. You get a whiff, enough to keep you going."

"It's torture, but not just torture", Neil responds. "The 'almost' almost drives me crazy. I don't give up on the sharing. It *is* possible. I've had it for moments. I want it as a central part of my life. It's not just control. It's more. And I want *more*."

Meanwhile, the new change continues. One more day his wife does not support the sharing feeling he is after—and he lets it go. He is amazed that this can happen and happen again. His wife somewhere else or nowhere bothers him, but the bother does not build and stop him cold. The disturbance does not block the flow of the day but is part of a moment. Unbelievably, the moment shifts, and he is in the next moment. It is difficult to appreciate the amazingness of this if you have not had to wrestle with the problem of letting go one state for another. The congealed sense of loss, disappointment, unfulfilment, accusation, injury, blame, instead of turning to paste and clogging emotional arteries, fades as the next thing happens. It dissolves in a general sense of well-being.

Neil wants the sharing with me too but tells me that the good feeling that supports him survives my not being there: "The other day I kept thinking I need you to validate this. I need you to validate this change is happening. But—it's real for me. A real shift. I'd love for you and my wife to 'get' it. But it's real for me. I tingle all over. What does it mean?"

"Hello", I say spontaneously.

"I guess that's what it means", Neil laughs.

After a silence, Neil speaks of a moment with one of his children. He tries to convince his boy that a certain activity would be good for him. Maybe Neil is right, maybe not, but it becomes clear that it is an activity that means something to Neil in terms of his image of what a child should be. "That's not who I am. I'm not that kind of person", his boy tells him. Neil feels proud and deeply moved. "I bathed in that remark", he says. "It was wonderful he could say that—such a gift. If I can take any portion of credit, I'll have done something significant with my life."

Sharing happens, but not as Neil expects. A child voices a difference that makes his heart sing.

* * *

Neil tells me that he and his wife had sex—astonishing news, since they rarely do. She will do it if he wants but goes through the motions as a peace gesture. She does not really like it, not with him, and has not for a long time. So he tries not to, holds out as long as possible. He wants to be wanted.

His wife changes the format by saying that this time she wants to pick the night. The idea seems mechanical to Neil, but he goes along with it, since it is a novel gesture on her part. He fully expects the night never to come, or, if it does, she will beg out or make it seem as if she forgot. But she picks a night, and it comes, and they have sex. The miracle is that they each have a shift of attitude.

He feels more open to whatever may or may not happen, and she tries an experiment with herself. She finds herself wondering what sex would be like with Neil if she regards it as play. In a moment the dichotomy between excitement and deadness drops away, and she is in a new field of experience. For the first time in years, she is in a place where she does not know beforehand what would or could happen with Neil, with her body, with self. She gives up control and feels her body a playground of possibilities, new mixtures of depth and buoyancy. A strange word to use but— she suddenly finds sex with Neil interesting, largely because she has hit upon an inner gesture that makes discoveries possible. Sex is better than ever, not because it is more exciting, maddening, even loving, but because it taps the unknown.

"There *is* life after death", I say.

"I'm going to be alive even if that sexual part of me is not as alive as I want."

The new feeling continues, spreads, claims territory. It invades sex, makes life bigger. His implicit frame of reference for what aliveness can be is shifting.

"It's the new feeling I've been telling you about", he says. "As I feel it, I feel my connection with my last, most maddening lover slip away. I feel my envy of her and her life, her experiences, slipping away. I feel a sense of deep relationship with my wife, a sense of deep relationship with myself. Just a month ago it did not seem possible. Now when I feel this feeling, the words come, 'How could your mother love you more? How could life love you more?' It may not make sense, but it's the way I feel.

"More words come. Something about the tangled web that perception weaves. There's something extremely distorting about accurate perception. Without ever knowing it in words, I had the sense: 'This is where she is, and she'll come back.' And she really came back!"

Neil's wordless sense that his wife would not stay shut down, that something more would happen with them, was part of the tangled web for years. Nothing was turning out as Neil envisioned, but the mute sense that *something would happen* proved accurate and worthwhile.

"A few nights ago she was sitting. I've always taken her sitting as oblivion, spacing out, nowhereland. I've never had much tolerance for it. Actually, I don't know where she goes or what is happening when she sits or if she is anywhere. For me it was always something to get her out of. I usually rasp, 'Are you OK?' This time I kissed her on her forehead and went about my business. I'm working on giving up the illusion of control. I felt happy then, letting her be, even if I kissed her.

"I get a sense I shut down in childhood in my way like she did and that's why we're together. By putting her down, I turn away my shut-down self. I try to turn off hints of it. Why does thinking about how shut down I've been make me happy? A month ago it would have been a ghastly thought, and now it is part of a good feeling."

Neil voiced awareness of a bond between Brenda and himself, something more than agreements or disagreements or even satisfactions and dissatisfactions. There was a deep sense of being they valued, even if, at times, it was placed in jeopardy.

* * *

Neil and Brenda have sex more often. Their sexual contact continues even after a family trip, which usually involves disappointments and collisions. "I'm accepting things as they come. Things are getting better with my wife. I don't have that kind of passionate attraction for her I once had and spent years trying to keep alive. It's a loss, but something's gained. I'm not stuck in disappointment, frustration, bitterness. It's lifted. I feel a sadness, but it's really OK. I'm finding love more."

That is, he is finding that there is more to love than was available to him before. Love keeps changing. He is less attached to an idea of love or a state believed to be love and more able learn more about the things love can be or turn into. After speaking about the more in love he stumbled upon, he speaks again of sex and the role it once played in his life.

"There are two kinds of sexual experiences for me. Body, psyche, heart contact all together, the way I hoped it would be. The way it was with my wife in the beginning and with my last lover. Then there's the split-off more purely sexual experience, an intrapsychic experience. Few people are attractive enough to reach this pure fantasy figure deep in my psyche, and I don't have a whole lot of desire for anyone else. Am I getting older? Where did my sex drive go?

"I had a fantasy that on my birthday my old lover would contact me, and she didn't. A possibly scheduled reunion slipped away. Actually, I was relieved. I wonder if some of the intense sexual stuff wasn't part of some intrapsychic skirmish? The more I feel alive, the less I need the purely sexual way, the concentrated place where I felt able to live, free to be me, totally stripped down.

"I can't believe our family trip turned out as well as it did. It was OK for my wife, my kids, for me. No skirmish floored us. A feeling I have with you seems to be carrying over. Part of my fantasy with you is I could say let's just go somewhere and see where it goes, and you will. It's about being able to see and follow the horizon line."

"Neil" and "Milton"

Neil is in touch with ways he is opening. Milton is more in touch with ways he keeps closing. He cannot bear the reality of being a hate-filled monster. For Neil, love is real, but his ideas of love are too controlling. It was as if he had known what love should be ahead of time. The idea that love itself might have a lot to teach him is something he is learning. He finds real satisfaction in the pain of learning. Milton annihilates every wave of love with suspicion and iron dedication to an awareness of all that is not love. Neil knows that much of personality is not loving, but he exquisitely values the mustard seed involved with love. Milton cannot value the little point of love because so much works against it.

Milton excruciatingly pinpoints ways love is exploited and is exploitative. Love is an excuse for ego getting its way, a sneaky bid for domination. Love is almost always hypocritical. Yet he recognizes that his wife and children are not hypocritical. Not all love is unreal. The fact that he sees this dangles an impossibility in front of him, since *he* will never love without hypocrisy. Yet this is precisely what he *must* do.

After years of expressing hate, Milton wonders what good it does. Yet he cannot stop hating. His sense of infancy or childhood is very alive: "I want to maim and possess my parents, but I am dependent and have to hold back. The truth is even if I try with all my might I will fail. It is not something one can do, totally dominate another person, totally possess another. I scream, kick, trick—the other is still other.

"The only integrated experience I have is hate. It is not even directed at them. I can't bring myself to direct it at them. The feeling in the whole of my body is: I hate her.

"I thought when you acknowledge these feelings and face them others come or they diminish or change. *But there are no other feelings.* Yet I'm not the kind who can get a gun and shoot people.

"The people who shoot others or put others down or go around being injurious—they think they're in touch with themselves. If you shoot someone or put down Jews or blacks or women or gays or foreigners—you feel in touch with yourself. My mind tells me you're not in touch with yourself. I'm in touch with my hate and try not to act on it. I try to shield others from it, although I know it's impossible. I try with all my might to be in touch with myself. But when I hear of killing or injuring—I think, they're in touch and act on it, and I hold back. I don't value my holding in as an action. I value it but don't feel it's as real. The whole hate thing is the real thing and that is unreal. I struggle to be in touch with more even if I fail. That used to be enough, but no longer. I don't think I can stand this much longer. But I come here and fight to feel a little and am torn down the middle, alone with this.

"Is the rage to destroy injected at birth? How is it passed on? I think they must have blown me apart, left me to die on the battlefield, only I survived. I survived as enemy, monster, destroyer. I survived and wish I hadn't. Beyond the sheer force of moving forward, life's demand to be lived, there is nothing that draws me, informs me, just hate, black, bitter, which I regard all around me. You can see me as sensitive to the dark side or a coward holding on to people, pretending to be good, clinging. When I was a child, I saw what life would be like alone and drew back. I refuse to let you go, even if you're not helping me.

"Something makes me tell you I know there are changes. I'm afraid for you to feel you haven't helped me, but I shouldn't have to say this. You shouldn't have to know or be told. It is enough for me to tell you that nothing is different even if I know there are changes and know there aren't."

There have been changes in Milton's life, but are they enough or the right kind? He has more material comforts and pleasures than he could allow earlier, more contact with loved ones, more growth professionally. But what he must come and tell me is that only hate is real (even if love is a force in his life). He must not let up if he is to feel that truth exists in this world at all. Yet he is aware that his truth kills truth. It is not a bind he can get out of. He must keep rushing into it, hitting it full force, breaking all his bones against it. He needs another who hears the realness of what he needs to say and of what he dare not or cannot say. Perhaps he wants to say how bad life is, how false and cruel and hurtful people are. But he says this over and over, and the world does not change. Perhaps what he wants to say can neither be said nor heard and, because of that, is all the more important to communicate, to somehow share.

* * *

Neil does not or cannot or need not reach full-scale awareness of how damaging ties are. He feels the work of damaged bonds in other ways. At first, he sees damage in others, not in himself. He does not understand how he gets so tied to damaged people (Milton is acutely aware that those closest to him now are less damaged than he). Only gradually does Neil glimpse the ways that he is not exempt, that damaging processes touch him too, and that he contributes to the passing on of damage in spite of himself.

Neil has areas of openness and wants to be as alive as possible: he is dedicated to aliveness. His controlling streak works against what he most wants. With precise logic, choices in life force him along paths he would not have picked if he knew better. But it is precisely conundrums that bedevil him that push him to new places.

Neil and Milton share a certain purity. Milton's vision of blackness is lily-white, uncompromising. Neil's sense of life's (partly his own) goodness is unshakeable. Both are challenged to let in perceptions of processes that do not succumb to what reality has taught them. The realness of living forces them beyond lenses they almost squeeze life into. Both have visions of goodness and light that inspire and depress them. Both want life to be better than it is. Both want it to be true. Both know that this is possible because Life *is* better than it is, better than true.

Sometimes I feel the Miltons and Neils of this world specialize in soul areas requiring particular kinds of labour. They approach difficulties we need to learn more about. Perhaps we, too, are specialists working in different domains with varying timetables for human usefulness, reaching for a human economy that is less harsh. There are moments I imagine Miltons and Neils and so many others pushing at the edges of what we experience, pressuring psyches to evolve in some way, finding more of what it is possible to find, stumbling over new ways to taste ourselves.

CHAPTER EIGHT

The need to kill oneself

The urge to kill oneself is more widespread than realized. It even may be a "normal" part of life. Freud (1920g) wrote of conflict between drives to die and live, a destructive drive aimed against self and displaced to others. To call the urge to kill oneself normal seems an exaggeration, a distortion. But it calls attention to an urge needing freer circulation in the psychic body.

"Ella"

Ella told me recently how good she felt after giving vent to the wish to kill herself. Such feelings were taboo to her. She fought them off as fast as possible when they entered awareness. Therapy gave her permission to express such frightening feelings as fully as possible.

As far back as Ella could remember, thoughts of suicide had been flickering on and off. They were momentary, sporadic, fragmentary, never a real possibility. But they frightened her, and she withdrew from them. Now, in therapy, she could feel her chest contract, hollow out, freeze, lose feeling. The frozen contraction spread through abdomen, genitals, limbs, even skin, up through shoulders, neck, inside her temples. Cheeks above, cheeks below tightened, clenched teeth, squeezed anus.

"I've been terrified of killing myself without knowing it. Thoughts of killing myself would come and go, and I recoiled from them. I didn't realize how tense they made me. It is as if I've been holding myself back from thinking them, as if I were afraid I'd actually do it."

Ella went on to explore how holding these thoughts back inhibited thinking in other ways—not only thinking, but feeling: "I can sense how a blank, knotted anxiety took the place of feeling nooks and crannies of myself. Instead of letting myself spread through my body, taste myself, I'd disconnect, grow numb, depressed, bleakly smile."

Ella's "bleak smile" bought her time and space. For example, her mother took this "smile" to mean that everything was all right, she was a good mother. Her boyfriends took it to mean that she liked them. No one seemed to notice that her smile meant that she was tense and frozen, buried in a stiff cocoon. No one seemed to care, as long as they got enough of what they wanted from her.

"No wonder I thought of killing myself. I get the idea now that maybe I wanted to die to see if anyone would know I was missing. There *are* ways I died. To be afraid to think thoughts and feel feelings is a kind of dying. My smile is a kind of suicide. I buy people off with it, hide behind it. But something happens to me when I'm hiding. I begin to fade away, disappear, as if watching myself dying while standing in place. I think of the Cheshire cat. All that's left of death is a sickly grin, sky-writing thinning out. I watch myself dying until I can't see the dying any more.

"I say I kill myself by turning off. Actually, it just happens—I can't really say I'm doing it. Now I tell you something about it. But it just happens. I happen to be there, then turn into not being there. I can say something about the turning because we're talking, because you let me feel it, you let me notice. It's something that comes about naturally, this freezing, tightening, vanishing. It's so natural I don't notice it. I never spoke about it or let myself in that it was happening."

Therapy gives people time and space to notice ways that suicide happens as they go on with their lives. Nearly entire lives can be a kind of suicide. Some people feel in more active control and speak of killing off thoughts, feelings, self. Some feel more passive and in awe of processes beyond control. It is a disturbing fact that a life can go on without a person occupying it.

Ella came to sense active and passive tendencies of self inextricably mixed. She sensed ways she was there and not there, and part of not being there involved suicidal needs. To gain access to the need to kill oneself as part of living can be an achievement. It makes more mental and emotional space available. As Ella put it: "I have more room to stretch. I'm a little less paralysed by the fact of being me. A little less paralysed by paralysis."

"Nick"

Nick, in contrast to Ella, was a control freak, obsessed with being an active agent. Will and power were crucial to him. He needed to be top dog in personal interactions and could not bear being passive. He feared being dominated and associated passivity with subservience. After some time in therapy, he blurted out: "Passivity is a kind of suicide."

At the same time, Nick struggled for many years with alcohol and drug abuse. It did not seem to dawn on him that taking drugs provided an outlet for passive needs. He left no room for passivity with people or even with himself but was overwhelmed by addictive tendencies. His passive side got its due with a vengeance. The black inference did not escape him: "Drug addiction is a kind of suicide too."

Gratification of passive needs underlies many suicides. Recently, there was a news story about a high-school star who doused himself with gasoline and burnt himself to death. Everyone described him as active, happy, involved—a young man who had everything. Among my many thoughts was the notion that he went to an extreme to get some down time.

There were periods during which Nick battled ideas of suicide. That he refused to give in reinforced his sense of agency: he was master of his life. Similarly, he looked to therapy to support his active force in relation to addictive tendencies. Therapy should help him gain strength to break the hold that drink and drugs had over him. Therapy should increase control and power over life and self.

For Nick, suicidal thoughts were associated with weakness. Weakness was something to push past, disregard, not give in to. By following this line of reasoning, "cure" was again in the ability not to give in to himself (not to give to himself?), growth in self-with-holding.

Nick was asking me to help him ignore passivity and not pay a heavy price. Suicidal urges contain a mix of active/passive tendencies. There is doer and done to, one part stifling, knocking out, annihilating another. The blind rage of the doer is unimpressed by the likelihood of disappearing with the whole personality. "If I can't be top, no one can." My personality = everyone's. "I'd rather kill myself than be passive." That is, I'd rather die than be no one.

If Nick had to kill himself, an active suicide would be better than a passive one. For a person addicted to the active side of personality, it seems better to take control of life and death. In Nick's case, however, suicide was viewed as a defeat, and Nick could not give up the idea of victory. The compromise his personality worked out was the quasi-suicide of substance abuse. Suicidal urges, too, played themselves out in making and losing fortunes.

After several years of therapy, Nick could say: "It hits me that repeatedly losing the money I make is a substitute suicide. Instead of killing myself like a man and ending the whole thing, I lose what I make. Instead of killing myself, I blow my money and mind to oblivion. It enables me to go on living. Why I want to, I don't know. I guess I feel that actually dying would be the biggest defeat of all, the greatest humiliation. I refuse to die but blow a fortune or my mind away instead."

Money becomes a substitute for life and self. Gain and lose money = gain and lose life and self. There seems, too, to be a hidden link between money, drugs, and alcohol: substances that not only alter consciousness, but stand in for it.

Little by little it began to dawn on Nick that I was not going to help him to become an even more completely active agent. In a moment of clarity he mocked me: "So, you refuse to make me into the Aristotelian God [pure activity, rationality]. You are a Taoist at heart." "Yes", I murmured. "You found me out. A Taoist at heart."

It was not before five years of therapy that Nick and I could articulate something like the following: "To the totally active god-you, passivity represents a kind of suicide. Pure activity as an ego-ideal would have to be relinquished or modulated. To the ego this seems like a failed attachment, a bet that has turned out badly. How can one give up on being a totally active god? What would it mean to be a God who makes room for rest? What would it mean to be a God who needs a Sabbath point of the soul?"

God is dead—long live God. There is a rhythm, like pulse-beats or breathing, active/passive, suicide/return. Nick was finally beginning to get the idea that something was missing in what failed to be a rhythm of active/passive tendencies. His life intermittently fell through a trapdoor in his psyche because it could not rest moment to moment. Nick had to blow himself away with drugs or loss in order to take time off from self.

A number of intertwining possibilities emerged:

1. suicide = diminution of activity as an ideal;
2. suicide = over-success of activity in killing off passivity;
3. suicide = rise of passive feelings and pleasures;
4. suicide = modulation of one-sidedness by emergence of blends or rhythmic pulsations or oscillations of mixed tendencies (death = diminution or lessened attachment to one-sidedness).

For example, Nick could not bear fellatio performed on him. It absolutely terrified him. He could not entertain being in such a passive position or enjoying passive pleasures. The times he tried to let a woman suck him, he had to stop it, literally terrified of dying (blow job, blown off, blown away, blowing with the wind). To enjoy being fellated would amount to a kind of suicide. He would have to undergo suicide before passing to the other side (heavenly bliss). He had some dreams of sucking himself off, and it occurred to him that that is what he did, in part, by taking drugs and alcohol. He sneaked in passive ecstasies only by maintaining some semblance of control (doing it to himself).

Eventually, Nick tried to describe what he felt when drugged or drunk out of his mind and he got an inkling that passive needs were being gratified in these states. Self-destructive activity—in a warped, injurious way—brought him towards a part of life that needed contact. Getting support to describe such states enabled him to begin to take in the fact that suicide has its pleasures. The link between suicidal urges and passivity was strong, but difficult for Nick to grasp. By emphasizing strengths and shutting out what he most feared, Nick lived on highly reduced wave-lengths, in spite of apparent successes.

Therapy provides an opportunity to practise suicide in semi-manageable doses. Mini-suicides are parts of sessions. There are moments in sessions when self dies out, mind goes blank, one chokes on self, paralysis, non-being. For Nick, such pauses were intolerable. He could not stand silence, incipient helplessness. He did not know how to wait. His was a "can do" attitude, which worked well enough in business but reached a wall when it came to self. Losing everything financially and narcotic highs-and-stupors (at once heightening/nulling) substituted for a capacity for silence. If life is a roller-coaster ride, for Nick the down was as important as the up, except the meaning of his downs went unrecognized. That his downs (loss of money, mind, self) contained a throttled, precious capacity seemed inconceivable.

In the course of downs, Nick lost his marriage and family. In spite of an ability to rise to the top, Nick succeeded in proving to himself that he was a failure, a non-entity, a nothing. During a recovery period, he sought therapy. "I've had enough. I'm scared, raw. I can't keep doing this. I'm not so young any more. My body is aching. I don't think I can take another fall." Nick was brokenhearted, appalled with his life, yet still smug. He wanted to do away with down without taking in its messages. Therapy was to help him not fall down again. Therapy was to help him with the ache while keeping him above the descent.

Nick's downs finally hurt enough for him to admit that something bad was working in him and that it was not going away—it was getting worse. His downs pushed him into therapy. Nevertheless, even if down and out, someone like Nick tries to get on top of therapy. He automatically tries to control the agenda, the scope, and means of sessions. Nick started therapy at the beginning of a new rise. I saw him just after his lowest point. "This time it's got to be different", he said. "This time I've got to succeed." It would seem that Nick was finally hurt enough to try something a little differently. Still, he filled therapy up with his drive for success, an almost certain recipe for failure. He simply did not know how to make room for therapy, nor make room for himself. He needed to take so much space that he left himself out.

It took less than a moment to sense that Nick could not know I was with him. Perhaps I was the audience—the one who hears, applauds, affirms. But who was supposed to hear? I did not feel it could be me. Perhaps I was someone to manipulate, a fellow technocrat or businessman or problem-solver—someone who treats problems like a contract to be worked out. The latter might require creative negotiations and be a start. But there was no room for fathomless beings together, infinitely subtle, variable subjective centres with awesome nuances, magnificent, lethal, dreadfully everyday.

There he was, Nick in my office, talking, talking, talking: "I this . . . I that. . . ." He seemed to be pushing himself away, pushing me away. An extroverted force. His focus was on the outside, on what happened to him, the rush of events, rise and falls of fortune, what he did, what he did again. And what he did to himself. But where was the self this was done to? I could feel him feel a sliver of the doer and feel part of the pain of the results. But I could not feel him feeling himself through and through. Pushing out, pushing away—that's what came across most forcefully.

My vision sifted through layers of pain, layers of fracture. I saw the scars of so many psychic shocks, strokes, heart attacks, many of which were still going on. How can a person be having a psychic heart attack or stroke while talking a mile a minute? How can someone be in shock while performing high-level financial dealings with hyper-speed mind. I did not know the stories of all the strokes, shocks, heart injuries—but I saw them inscribed in the tightness of his body, the expulsive fury of his mind. I felt undersides long buried, hardened, transcended, outgrown. The room silently teemed with children of his soul in scorched playgrounds turned to graveyards. The maimed unborn, throttled, helpless.

Many murders, suicides. The more he talked, the more I heard death below the surface.

"I'm killing myself to stop getting murdered. It's not just that being murdered would be too passive. I imagine taking charge in some way would limit the pain." I'm hallucinating my patient. My versions of Nick proliferate. "I kill myself and come back, determined to make good, to be a winner." Nick refuses to be kept down. He leaves the corpse of himself behind, aborts suicides, stamps on his souls, rides mind fragments to victory. He steps over many corpses of self but slides through holes of all that disappeared.

I became watchful, shut out by Nick's stream of words. Did I think my silence was good for him? Was I being mean, withholding, afraid, withdrawn, repulsed, vengeful? To be too silent too long can starve a person. I could not let him fall forever through the empty space of his words. If I spoke, I felt my words bounce off him or vanish in the barrage of sounds they triggered. With guilty curiosity, I became aware of tuning Nick out: "My God, I'm committing a kind of suicide."

I watched ways I killed myself off. You cannot be sure of catching the moment. You may not see yourself at the moment of death: "It happened. I missed it again. I'm not here. I vanished and didn't see myself vanish. And now I can only come back partly. I cannot retrace the vanishing. Reappearing cuts another path." It is a little like a limb that has gone to sleep, and you have to wait for the pins and needles to disappear, but you know you are there, your limb is slowly recovering, you will soon be flesh and blood again. The flow of blood to consciousness can be cut off. Your inner position cuts the flow, and you move a bit mentally as you await your return.

I have inklings of some of my therapeutic biases, but most are probably beyond my reach. One well-practised fantasy involves the notion that I am entering a state relevant to Nick. It is not just my personal difficulty that I commit suicide in sessions. Yes, if I were a bigger person, better, more evolved, fuller, more robust—I might not have to die. I could remain related, I would not withdraw or disappear. That would be an ideal me, someone I am not. It is often the case that committing suicide and being murdered are fused. It is possible that Nick is murdering me, and I take control of my passivity by imagining I kill myself. It is possible that I simply am not enough of a person for Nick.

Right or wrong, I develop the conviction that my having no room for myself in sessions is relevant to Nick's not being available to himself or to me. If Nick relates in a way that drives me to suicide, perhaps my death reflects his own. If I have no room for feelings, perhaps Nick has no room for feelings. There is no room for feelings in the space we do not share—or, rather, what is shared is the state of there being no room. Therapy becomes a shared suicide. A shared mutual occlusion.

What I take in is Nick's partial evacuation of self. Ways he gets rid of himself get under my skin. The fact that I get rid of myself under the impact of his getting rid of self is something I become aware of over time. I gradually sense that I go under, grow numb, lose attention, blur out—lose consciousness. Loss of consciousness and self becomes an object of consciousness and self. Nick and I become mirror images of self-murder. The fact he does most of the talking and I become the guardian of silence make us something like positive and negative images in a stuffed/starved dying space. It is possible for space to commit suicide too.

I must face up to my guilt. There is a kind of self-attack that masks deeper possibilities of dying. I must not let the fact that I am not more of a person stop me from honouring the stunted reality Nick and I live together. We are truncated beings together and must do nothing to rob ourselves of disability. Therapy itself is a damaged bond but hopefully also a healing one. We live a disabled reality, but we can do so more or less honourably, fully, truly.

If I am exposed to Nick's impact, he is exposed to mine. If we constitute disabled space together, our parts are not identical. He is more talkative, I more silent. I cling to silence as if preserving an endangered species. There are silences that lead to or result from mental/emotional suicide. But there are silences that preserve something precious.

Much goes on in silence. Nick showers words on me and withholds himself. Nick-feelings grow inside me. So many Nick-images begin to meld and play off each other. I have my own deepening/widening internal Nick pool. The very fact that I am dying out, that he pushes me out, pushes himself out, that I push him/me out—a place in me becomes reserved for him, if only, at first, this pushing-out feeling. But this pushing-out feeling is only the tip. It leads elsewhere. As I feel and meditate on the pushing-out feeling, I become aware that it is impacted, dense. This seems strange at first because the spray of his words, with all their hammering quality, becomes diffuse: on the one hand diffusion, on the other density.

Dualities like diffusion/density can be confusing, and I feel a tendency to want to simplify them, to grab hold of them. It is impossible to let them be and follow them without altering them, making them into something I can think. Yet I do feel it true that Nick is confused by his own being, at once diffuse and impacted. I get the distinct sense that he tries to hold himself together by pushing himself out. He is identified with ambition and power, mystified by loss and self-destruction. As I sense the him outside/ inside me, I feel a compressed, knotted being, so tightly held for so many years that the self-holding, self-tightening is scarcely accessible. It is nearly as much a part of him as breathing.

I can feel the contraction in his/my chest, abdomen, groin, shoulders, neck—a boa coiled within, squeezing and suffocating itself. There is, too, hardness that keeps getting harder, flakes off, crumbles, hardens as it crumbles, crumbles as it hardens. When I feel Nick in me, my body crumbles/hardens.

I touch expulsion and find contraction; touch hardness and find diffusion. In imaginary vision I move through the Nick in me like a slowly moving diver, tracing tensions, openings. I see the painful underside of Nick's face, and my face reflects the pain. I look like he unconsciously feels. My shoulders hunch, chest draws in, stomach squeezes, breath stops, drawing a shell of the body around anticipated pain that never stops.

I am the hunched, drawn-in one. His own body is assertive, charged, engorged. I preserve the traumatized self, loss, nothingness. Even in defeat, Nick is determined to be someone, to be big. I am his hollowed-out being filled with ever-crumbling/hardening cement, filled with the will to triumph. I am his defeated soul. His identity fills a vacuum hidden by life. He cannot take in that self-destruction is part of identity too. There is not much letting in.

Little by little, I see him seeing me out of the corner of his psyche. He is aware that I am there, whoever I am. I am someone not talking him out of himself, someone letting him fall. He cannot get rid of the him-in-me with words. He is perplexed and curious about being part of my inner life. It is strange for him to find himself inside me. It is something new to bump up against another's quietness and find the quietness moulded around himself.

He begins to notice that he is internally alive for me and that the him-in-me is more complex and unknowable than what he is used to calling himself. He cannot alter the fact of silence, of thought, of his seeping into my inner world. This can be terrifying—akin to dread of soul captured by a photo or mirror, but also freeing. He is not an inanimate image but a growing presence in a living being.

How can he be inside me without dominating me? How is it possible to be in each other in ways neither of us can control? What dies is self-encapsulation, the determination to live without being inside an other. What grows is the sense that one is more than one imagined, and so is everyone else.

Nick began feeling suicidal as self-encapsulation began to break up. He began feeling the limitations of his domineering ways and lacked resources to fall back on. One may come alive in new ways before one is ready to.

"Suicide, like murder, is never-ending", are words that came to me. One needs both soul movements. Nick could not access either. They possessed him through reversals of fortune. Up on top involved murder of the other, down on bottom involved murder of self. In life, such movements follow each other. In psychic reality, they coincide or work simultaneously. Language and time and circumstances require spread.

What would Nick be like if he could glimpse soul murder (of self or other) as an ongoing event, as something real?—as something worth time and effort and consideration? What would happen if he saw what he was doing by pushing himself away? Could he see what he lost by needing to take charge?

The fact that he saw me working on him in myself gradually seeped in. He could not stop himself from being interested in the him in me.

Many suicides and murders are involved in breaking up hardened slivers of identity. Worse suicides and murders may be involved in holding on to identity crusts or cores long past their time.

One thing that dies somewhat is the idea that I can live my life without being uncontrollably alive in someone else and *vice versa*. To begin feeling the unknowable me in another arouses a new sense of the other in me. Shocks of disintegrating self-formations coincide with shocks of being touched by life anew.

Nick commits suicide as I murder him, and I commit suicide as he murders me. What dies, partly, is self-encapsulation. What lives is mutual permeability. However, encapsulation never ends, nor is suicide or murder ever complete. Relationships between encapsulation and permeability evolve as life turns another face. Same old me in a different God. Same old God in a different me. Both of us in a somewhat different place.

* * *

Mystical language can be very aggressive. The nuclear paradox of dying to be reborn is basic. We are very much in process of discovering new turns of this challenging truth.

Jesus brings the sword, not only peace. "The violent shall bear it away." Aggressive energy is needed to crack the shell of heaven, to crack the shell of self. The creative, loving God employs immense destructive energies. Prophets tell us to cut open our hearts—an inner circumcision that sensitizes an invisible organ whose pulse may never stop. There are Hindu deities who specialize in necessary destruction.

There is much violence against others and much violence against self. Mystical life takes hold of this violence and blows open pathways towards God. Self-destruction seeks the Sabbath point of the soul.

Cracking the heart, shattering the self, breaking the mirror, crushing the grapes, grinding glass or wheat—are some images of self-grinding aiming at inner freedom.

"Never stop dying", I recently said to a man who felt that the state he sought eluded him. His face lightened, and he expressed relief. A sense of inadequacy had been compounded by not being able to break through in a final way. He had been fearful of taking the next step, and the step after that—perhaps because it would only be another step. Weeds grew faster than paths cleared. Now he saw that the programme was bigger, and what steps he took were all he had.

People need permission to lacerate themselves, kill themselves over and over. Perhaps they try to rub stain out of soul. Cut sin out of life. Do away with the thing that feels wrong or off. They fail but open new territory in the cutting. There is too much pressure to be good to self, not enough support for ripping self apart. Not enough support for finding what is left after the ripping or the regions that appear between tears.

Oedipus tears at his eyes. It is the eyes of his soul he is after. No amount of self-blinding can find absolute darkness. Yet pride of eyes lessens, and other regions open.

Biblical destruction is taken for granted. The question is only who will get destroyed. Can one by good deeds deflect destruction from oneself? Or will the sum of sin collapse in on itself? The psalmist incessantly entreats God to keep destruction out there, on the enemy. He hopes that his innermost bond with God, his faith, will be protection. He knows that there is enough evil in his heart to warrant disappearance in a flash, but his inner God-bond, a deeper heart, opens other worlds of experiencing.

> How precious to me
> are thoughts of You, God
> how overwhelming their beginnings.
>
> [Psalm 139.17]

Thinking of God is thrilling—the bond of bonds. Let wrath be for the wicked beyond this bond. Today we might say, let wrath do its work on our evil inclination, enabling a precious heart connection to shine more brightly.

At the Passover seder we invoke Elijah in rage against our enemies, those who injure us throughout the ages. But we also ask Elijah never to stop cleansing us. No one gets to the bottom of guilt or ends self-injury. We can never do ourselves in enough to be pure. Not even Elijah can cut out the necessary warp.

But we keep cutting. Deeper incisions. Regions of being open. We go further into God-bonds. We did not know that being alive could feel this way, and this, and this.

Psychoanalysis speaks of reversal of affect. Aggression cuts both ways: self ↔ other. The self-immolation of the Desert Fathers, the skinning of Rabbi Akivah—we continue this movement inside us today. We also try to gain advantage over others, control their destinies, take their goods, enhance our own position as we imagine it. It matters a great deal to individuals to what extent aggression is turned outward or inward. For the human race as a whole, aggression is variably distributed, shifts forms, changes with circumstances.

Therapy is a microcosm of society, cells in larger bodies. We see how aggression distributes itself moment to moment, now aimed at self, now aimed at others. The deepest bonds call forth the most aggression, at the same time the latter is incessantly displaced. A perennial problem with aggression is that wherever it goes, it boomerangs. No movement is final. There is always recoil. We cannot predict where it lands next, only that direction changes.

The most self-hating people see the worst in others as well. They rightly complain they are deprived of affectionate contact. But whoever comes near them risks getting skinned.

How does one turn self-hate into something useful? To what extent can this happen? To what extent is self-hate and its transforms necessary?

We must make room for aggression against the self—in extreme form, the impulse to kill oneself. It continues its work whether or not we make room for it. We keep ripping at what pains us. We take inner baths, try to clear away barriers. If we fail to see that movement against self has value and importance, we may do ourselves and others real harm. Soul rubs and shines itself by immolation/demolition, a capacity we are ever in danger of using against ourselves and others. We must learn to kill ourselves without end without doing ourselves real injury. We may discover ways of "killing" ourselves that make us better people.

CHAPTER NINE

Tinkering

Does it make sense to make sense of a life? One constructs frames of reference, ways of thinking about a life that include social, political, psychological aspects of history. One finds ways to understand. Still, life sifts through one's fingers, like sand, and one wonders at the fleeting nature of time. One wonders at capacities we discover, our makeup, our use and misuse of all we are given, its use and misuse of us.

"Sam"

Sam tells me that he is brilliant then spills out his story of damage. He depicts his mother as seductive, father as rageful, both as depressed. His father's depression is lifelong and powerful, his

---

From *fort da*, 5 (1999): 64–83. Reprinted with the permission of the Northern California Society for Psychoanalytic Psychology.

mother's was more serious when he was a child, lessening as he grew up. Sam felt that he saved himself by being super-smart and great at everything. He was athletic, social, a terrific student. He got into top schools, flew through graduate school, got an amazing job making lots of money, terrific girlfriends, wonderful friends.

Why does he seek me?

He is very lonely. He likes having girlfriends and lots of money but wants to build a life with a special someone and have a family. He wants a substantial life, someone to love who loves him and work he really loves. He is good at creating a terrific but loveless life. Love, like time, is elusive.

Sam is expert at rising above himself and his circumstances after sinking for a time. He turns out screenplays, songs, poems, he runs through relationships, jobs, he gets drunk a lot, he runs through years. He hopes to make enough money to quit loveless jobs and write. His approach to writing is as addictive and orgiastic as everything else—orgasmic bursts, followed by drops into nothingness. He lacks staying power. He cannot tolerate sustained, persistent effort. He drops whatever he does.

Sinking into something, dropping it, rising above it blend and blur. I get the sense that Sam carries his capacity for transcendence too far, that it has taken an exasperating twist. After successfully transcending (in some way, to some extent) parental rage, insecurity, and depression, he goes on transcending everything that comes his way, everything he dips into, everything that threatens to pull him in. He is so afraid he will sink and drown in something bad that he has become addicted to rising above himself, letting go whatever builds. Truth is, he may be even more terrified of drowning in something good, even though there is nothing he wants more.

Sam claims to be devoted to Beauty. He needs beautiful women, literature, art. Twice since I have known him he has approximated something like falling in love. Two women struck him to the core. He cannot have this feeling if a woman is not beautiful. He insists that the special someone he spends his life with must be beautiful in a way that not only quickens his soul but rings his bells so tellingly that he feels close to God. Sam describes the Beauty he has in mind as a kind of cosmic force, God's beauty incarnate in Woman, uniting him with the Truth and Goodness of Life, his life, his destiny, his spiritual power and viability, the very truth of life itself.

Both relationships were volatile. The first, with "Elise", lasted longer. It reached the point where Sam and Elise could not spend an hour together without furious recoil, no matter how they tried. Sam felt that he could make it with Elise. She could be a lifelong partner. He felt soul glow with her. He looked at her and saw God. But she felt controlled by him and flew into rages. She felt used for her God value, not seen for herself. Her own sense of self was challenged by abusive roots, so that a wrong look aroused suspicion, accusation, emotional storms. She could not take another's demands, and Sam's seemed extraordinary. The intensity that attracted her made her fight like mad.

It took time and much talk before Sam could begin to see his contribution to the disaster. He did not think that his needs should blow Elise's fuses. She should be able to respond more openly, fully. For a while, he bent over backward trying to respond to her, making space for her, taking her sensitivity into account. Nothing worked. Exasperation and injury fuelled each other. Finally, they could not be with each other.

He felt justified in the years following the break-up when his life advanced and Elise's dropped to lower levels. He was able to do more with himself than she with herself, so it seemed. Sam insisted that he could have made it with her if she had been able to make it with him—if only the impact of beauty had been backed by a personality strong enough to support it. For years, Sam hoped that Elise would develop to the point where they could be together. But that kind of growth never occurred. Elise did not catch up, and Sam was left to mourn the loss.

The next "truth" relationship was short-lived. Fighting started almost immediately. Again, the woman, "Lou", was emotionally volatile. Her beauty sliced through Sam, and he enjoyed her liveliness. Both felt the other did not give enough. By the time Sam began to open up more, Lou was out the door. Surprisingly, months later they became friends. A friendly relationship survived the explosive one. Once more Sam felt loss—so near, so far. He was convinced that he could have made a go of it if *she* could: again, a woman's failure, but he was beginning to wonder.

Why was his attachment to beauty so explosive? He was struck by beauty that blew up in his face, that blew up in his heart.

* * *

There came a time when I could point to Sam's cutting off when I was faulty. This sounds odd, since we are always faulty. But sometimes flaws are more bothersome. At moments my insensitivity seemed *too* unpalatable. He withdrew around his sensitivity, silent wrath insulating injury. Sam scowled contemptuously, giving up on me—why should he relate to a lower vibratory creature, a gross being lacking awareness of his subtle nature. I ought to realize that nursing a grudge was a way to lick a wound.

Such contempt-tinged formulation was the tip of it. Neither of us saw how derailed he really became. When I lacked sensitivity, to his sensitivity he fell off the earth, spiralled through pain into endless nowhere, falling through worlds of agony into numbness. He became unreachable. When he looked at me, he saw someone who did him wrong, someone to retreat from.

With girlfriends he broke the fall by lashing out to regain control. Through rageful argument he tried to convince them to be responsive, to own their injurious ways. He tried to get them to nurture him. He tried to get them to talk about their feelings and see things his way. Each pushed his/her position, nursing injury with furious righteousness.

Since I did not sleep with him, there was less at stake with me. Since he came to me for help, there was more at stake. Since he would never marry me, there was less at stake. Since he needed to get better in order to marry, there was more at stake.

Perhaps he felt that I was trying to get him to talk about feelings and see things my way. Perhaps he felt I was lobbying for psychoanalysis with him, that I did with him what he did with girls.

When I suggested that he felt in danger of being brain-washed by me as he brain-washed his girlfriends, he indignantly insisted that he was just trying to get a woman to respond to him. He just wanted someone to be open and honest. Why did it always degenerate into a battle for control?

Perhaps all he wanted was a therapist who could respond to him too.

* * *

We passed through many hellish moments when I precipitated hurt, angry withdrawal, grudging wound nursing.

We eventually came back, resurfaced.

I was not as fiercely reactive as his girlfriends, or, at least, I did not have an urge to give in easily to my flagrant reactivity. His withdrawal, fall, furiously anxious control triggered my awareness of similar emotional processes in myself. What he went through was far from unknown to me. I felt my sensitivity, pain, withdrawal, fall—they were states I worked with for years. In a way, he was a familiar version of myself. But I did not feel the need to go through these feelings in as total a way as he did, at least not with him. They passed through my awareness in a less full-blown and raw way.

I do not think I tried to control him as much as he did his girlfriends (but I cannot be sure). I did not hold on to him as desperately, nor detach myself as acutely. A difference was my concentration on the painful falling itself, without grabbing on to anything except concentration on the fall. Sam could see me concentrating (or trying to) on what was happening between us. He could see me immersed in following what happens in the fall, the need to right oneself (be right), the inability to do so.

What I am describing is a kind of resonant miniaturization in myself of what Sam went through in a fuller way. The same painful withdrawal, hurt rage, despair at ever being met by someone—I could feel it in myself, cushioned by compassion that has grown over years, deepening awareness of suffering we go through, often inflicted by our own makeup.

Compassion grows around withdrawal. And while pain drives us back from each other, Sam feels me working with the pain in myself. One does not have to be so totally tyrannized by pain, injury, personal injustice. Sam sees me cushioning in myself the pain he feels. What we do to each other does not have to end the link between us, although the latter is threatened for a while.

When Sam was hurt by me and went into a spin, he might say something like: "I'll never be open with you. Something clicked off. You're someone I have to watch out for. My feelings for you are damaged. We'll never connect. You blew it."

As time went on, he could say: "This is how I get with other people, especially girlfriends, even much worse. I stay like this until we blow up. I can't stop it. I can postpone it sometimes, then it blows. I've been like this all my life. I know it started with my parents. My father's like this. Maybe my mother too, although in a more complicated way."

A little understanding is something. But more important is actually going through the traumatic sequence in a new way. Sam and I kept working, returning to each other through the twists and turns of traumatizing moments. We went through the traumatized bond experience many ways, tasting now this aspect, then that. Through living it in somewhat attenuated form, it became a little more tolerable, bearable, digestible. Being done in from moment to moment was not something he had to be done in by. It was something he could live with, make use of.

Doing each other in is part of growing together. What we do with doing each other in determines how far we can go with each other.

* * *

It is terrible to live with the fear that at any moment the other cannot take us, that we cannot take ourselves. Yet this fear is all too prevalent. It marked Sam's life without him grasping it.

Sam knew that his mother was depressed, insecure, seductive, and that his father was depressed, rageful, and self-loathing. In one or another way, he had taken this into account since childhood. He fought against their weaknesses, rose above them, pushed past them, walled off from them. But his fight left him with the sense that at any moment he could step into quicksand. The sense of lacking support for one's capacities and being can take one off guard at any moment.

In psychoanalytic fantasy one imagines what it is like to be a baby with a loving mother who is fearful, seductive, depressed. One is loved and cajoled into being, only to suffocate in emotional smog, drown in fear, stolen from oneself by the other's need for justification. Real strength, affirmation, and pleasure mixed with dread, black holes, fragility, disability. The rage and glee of a self-hating father attempting to make his son bigger than life, magnified by injured need, shooting him down with missiles of crippled emotions. Each step is an adventure. One is ever launching oneself into life. One lifts a foot, flies to the heavens, but by the time the foot comes down, the earth is gone. Moments of well-being, strength, triumph, excitement are followed by loss, deadness, doubt, torment, fear, paralysis. Fold the two sides over so they coincide. Glory and futility permeate the same moment.

Is it simply that Sam is supersensitive to the vanishing moment? How does something build if one is ever vanishing?

Yet we do build—civilizations, art, governments, lives. How, Sam wonders, is this possible with integrity? Isn't everyone transfixed by the moment to moment flow? Isn't everything that is meaningful in one part of one's life meaningless in the next?

In spite of our failure, Sam and I continue. We persist through everything that he hoped therapy would be and is not. We persist, though whatever happens in a session vanishes by the next. Through fear, failure, rage, seduction, loss, suspicion, mistrust, hope—is a bond growing in the vanishing, a background sense of support?

* * *

It is one thing to have a handy cocktail-party narrative of one's life, yet another to truly feel what one talks about. Sam long sensed that his relational failures were linked with patterns laid down in childhood. But to taste the nuanced complexity of what he was up against was something new.

In Sam's case, results were multi-edged. Moment to moment reactions to injury in therapy opened the possibility of viewing and working with reactive injury patterns generally, particularly those that stymied living. Being injured is one thing. Compounding injury by one's reactions to injury is something therapy addresses. As we spent time together, Sam experienced how injury added to injury in reactive spirals. To see this repeatedly at work between us was astonishing enough. Even more astonishing was realizing the extent to which hardened injury patterns pervade day-to-day living across a lifetime.

To say that Sam picks women who are, in some ways, like his mother or father is not the same as the gut-wrenching, awesome living through of that fact or fantasy. Sam was totally aghast to see Elise collapse during the years after their relationship. He could scarcely believe how events unfolded. When they met, she had been beauty itself—striking, startling, searing. She was strong, vital, alive, brilliant. Elise was a part-time model, which titillated him, made her more desirable, but also elicited jealousy, fear. She was attractive to many, attracted by many.

The fear that at any time she might be someone else's lover drove Sam crazy and challenged him. It drove him to bind her to himself, to win what men desire. In old psychoanalytic parlour talk, he sought the other man's woman, the forbidden. In fact, Sam took Elise from another man and tried to make her his own.

Sam denied that the fantasy of another man's desire was crucial, that he imagined Elise as an object of all men's desire. Whose desire? Which man's desire? Sam did not like to think that his desire was a composite of many desires, many people's desires, desire made of many angles.

What was real for Sam was Elise's beauty, which Sam insisted was spirit beauty, at one with face and body beauty. Elise was an artist and poet as well as a model, and Sam fell in love with her artist's soul, her aesthetic sensibility. He did not think that pure physical impact alone would thrill him so deeply. It was who Elise was, as well as what she looked like, that mattered.

It was difficult for Sam to believe that he was seductive and controlling like his mother. What felt most real was pure soul feeling. Elise touched God and harmony and made being vivid. He could not comprehend her growing rage and expected it to pass. He tried to be less controlling and give her space. But the emotional forces and patterns played themselves out, and he and she were swept along. At times he saw her as his fragile mother, his raging father. He felt within himself the rage he hated in his father. He did not anticipate such fusion of the ugly and the beautiful.

Most devastating of all was the aftermath. During the years following their break-up, Elise became depressed, she stopped working, she could not take care of herself. Sam failed to digest the realization that fragility, depression, and collapse could be the other side of vitality, brilliance, and beauty. He could not believe the depression and fragility he thought he escaped staring at him from the hole of Elise's torment. He had imagined her invulnerable, transcendent. Mutual injury and rage covered the hole she disappeared into—the hole he had climbed out of since childhood.

He hated his mother for the support he had to give her in order for him to have enough of a mother to get through childhood. He had to nurse her emotionally in order for her to be somewhat there for him. He went through life being an emotional nurse hoping to be nourished. Elise's collapse, which was tragic enough, seemed an exaggerated version of his mother's infuriating fragility. It was hard to avoid seeing that he was magnetized by beauty that could not support him or itself. He gravitated towards a hole, a lack, a need—towards someone who needed the support he was hoping to find.

* * *

For Sam there is nothing more precious than beauty. The sense of beauty links with goodness and truth, the best life offers. It is the very core of life's intensity, the preciousness of experiencing. Beauty gives one faith in life and faith opens beauty.

If Sam is questioned about this, he insists that life would not be worth living if not for the beauty of creative joy. Creativity brings one to the edge of all one can be. The spontaneity of children touches this beauty, as does poetry, art, the mind and heart of friends. Women awaken a beatific tuning fork. When Sam speaks of his beauty feeling, he speaks, in his way, of the soul's communion with God.

When I push Sam, he insists that he does not at all mean to exclude nasty things, life's ups and downs, lows as well as highs. He means everything life offers, if not everything life demands.

I cannot avoid feeling that Sam over-idealizes life. Part of me thinks that he expects more than life can give. Another part thinks: "Good for him. Go for it, Sam." Why compromise prematurely?

Can youthful idealism take one all the way?

When must realistic love kick in?

He makes more money and has more beautiful women than I ever did. He must be doing something right. He must be better, more developed than I ever could be. Who am I to help him? Maybe he should be helping me?

On the other hand, I have dug in, grown roots, worked the trenches. I have a family with all its travails—something he thinks he wants, something he tells me he wants. I have been in the same crazy relationship with a woman (my wife) for more than two decades. Mine is all too real, sometimes radiant, filled with painful difficulties and challenges that would have sunk any relationship

Sam might have had. Sam had a cute *tabula rasa* face until very recently.

I have been working as a therapist for four decades, and the work keeps growing. Sam wants to quit work and write. He is trying to save enough money to do that. He is pretty close. Meanwhile, I keep translating bits of my work into books—messages in bottles, seeds of beauty and horror. Maybe someday his poems will grow in heart, as well as dizzy mind. Maybe his work will go further than mine. First he has to write it. First it has to come into being. The incommunicado vision must make contact with the world.

I remember a turning point, a moment over thirty years ago. I was writing and trying to put everything into it—Vision, Beatific Truth, *IT ITSELF*, the unsayable everything. In a semi-blackout I realized that no assault will get it right. If I am to survive as a writer, I must accept mortality, deficiency. Nothing I write will quite be It. What is on the page misses the mark in crucial ways— always something else, not It. To write at all, I must accept my death as a writer. By the time words reach the page, they are already rotting corpses. Whatever reaches the page is shot through with limit, deformation.

The amazing grace is that there are moments when It shines through, when It happens—life after death, through death. After giving up the ghost and surrendering or changing expectations, radiance passes from soul to soul.

Is it my job to shepherd Sam towards such a death? Can I know what his way must be?

People in his life tell him he is better, changing—whatever "better", "changing" means. There are moments we can feel each other when we are together, and feel each other feeling each other. We make eye contact with eyes that *can* make contact. Sam's skin seems softer, more complexly textured, more available. Moments of contact no longer only or mainly end with conflagration or irony or injured pulling back. We find new places by feeling each other out, by feeling the "feel" of what we are like together.

Yet Sam clings to beauty with all his psychic teeth. He refuses to be toothless. He will never give up.

The gap between ideal beauty and actual living is momentous. Sam is entering middle age, and he spends his time at work he

hates. He has had several decades to find ways to spend his time at
what he thinks he loves. He spends day after day at work he hates,
night after night with girls he will never love. Yet Sam says that he
wants to link up with what he loves with all his heart.

Will our time together help him to find the way to what he
loves? Is therapy one more thing he does not really want but endures, something he thinks he needs to do, should do? One more
alienating activity like those that have marked his path since childhood?

Will something happen between us that will enable him to
brave a fuller connection with himself? Will it happen soon? Is it
happening now? Is it building over time? Are new heart/head
connections already forming?

Will established patterns of mental control over injury reign,
damaged bonds deflecting love from work and people? Will he
continue to do what he does not like to do because a hidden sense
of injury is too great?

"Carrie" and "Marlene"

Carrie becomes a star. She works all her life to be recognized and
now is part of a hit show. She is in demand and works incessantly.
Her agent and husband push her to make one public appearance
after another. She has never been happier but is nagged by a sense
that something is wrong. She has no time for herself. She begins to
worry that by finding herself she is losing herself. She is, at once,
happy, anxious, jagged, empty, hollow. She fears disappearing in
the light.

Her therapist, Marlene, bolsters her, plays both ends. Marlene
supports Carrie to find more time in the face of demands of career,
agent, husband, self. She supports her in face of a destructive undertow that is hard to define. Marlene suspects that Carrie has
difficulty tolerating success. Perhaps Carrie feels that she does not
really deserve success and cannot let herself enjoy its fruits.
Marlene tries to work with Carrie's sense of guilt.

Carrie's low self-esteem, bad feelings about self, self-hate drive
her to achieve and undercut achievement—a variation on Sisy-
phus rolling the ball up, knocking it down. Habit and adaptation

level play a role. Carrie has worked for decades enjoying little triumphs amidst difficult times and injuries. A higher level of success overwhelms her. She needs to deal with new pleasures, possibilities, challenges. At the same time, good feelings about herself and life help her feel she is coming into her element. She, too, is star-struck with herself, in wonder and awe at what is happening to her.

With Marlene in her corner, Carrie began to find ways to make time for herself and deal with fame's demands and rewards. But just as things looked as if they were working out, Carrie became ill. She felt fatigue, which she managed to push past for a while. When she complained, her agent, husband, and others tried to get her to keep pushing. They felt it a matter of will or courage. She could beat it.

So often illness is looked at as something to fight. The idea that her growing inability to get out of bed might be telling her something was alien to her milieu. It was not a message anyone wanted to hear.

Doctors suspected a virus, but nothing was found. Some advised her to rest, some advised her to keep going as well as she could. Others advised combinations of work and activity, trial and error, whatever might work. Carrie missed engagements, cancelled shows. Those close to her began to panic. She was ruining the chance of a lifetime. Fury and concern mounted. They mounted attacks on her loss of energy and found ways to get her to work. Her ratings continued to rise.

She developed a colitis-like condition, at first weak and intermittent, then impossible to ignore. She could not trust her functioning. Pain was unpredictably consuming and diarrhoea uncontrollable. Even those closest to her, who most wanted her on stage, balked in face of an increasingly dangerous medical condition, although they pushed as much as they dared. At last the point came when Carrie could not leave her room.

Marlene called in guilty panic. She watched a successful therapy slip away. What had she done wrong? Was it her fault? Her contact with Carrie now was mostly by telephone. She was in terror of losing a patient who was losing her life.

Marlene, like Carrie, could not trust her own functioning. She tried to hold her patient in life, and now that life was failing. What kind of helper was she? Whatever she tried turned out wrong. Carrie's downhill spin made Marlene doubt her own therapeutic capacity. Something must be wrong with her as a therapist or therapeutic person if she failed so abysmally when success seemed so close.

Marlene readily admitted that she felt proud of her patient's success. Before therapy, Carrie had not been able to break through. Marlene felt proud of Carrie's fame, in which she could not help thinking, therapy had played a part. Therapeutic pride, like parental narcissism, can be a helpful and a dangerous thing.

To what extent did Marlene collude with Carrie's husband and agent, acting as a second between rounds in a prize fight, getting her ready for the next round? Even more devastatingly, was she like an old-time psychiatrist helping a battle-fatigued soldier go back to war? Marlene coached Carrie past bad feelings about herself, girding for victory. She thought that she sided with her patient's life; now she feared she had misjudged powerful and complex forces. She had been afraid to sense what her patient could not tell her.

Carrie's talent and drive to be successful are real. So is her drive to undo success. What goes into the latter? An ingredient in Carrie's case is the disparity between success as a disappointment and disappointments involved in struggling to be successful. Carrie was better able to deal with the latter. Once Marlene began speaking herself out, she quickly saw that she did not give Carrie a chance to explore how success failed her. Marlene was used to working with Carrie's sense of failure on the way up (the many falls, bruises, disappointments). She did not let in deeply and fully enough Carrie's unhappiness with success when it came.

The intensity of Carrie's disillusionment with success was obscured by the latter's benefits. The rush, the high of fame and achievement, recognition, excitement and clamour, easing of financial stress, no end of good work—what rude ingratitude not to appreciate the plethora of ways life opens. Can one be disappointed with a life that gives so much?

Did the glow of fame by proxy blur Marlene's vision, so she did not take seriously enough Carrie's doubts and counter-voices? Did reassurance and analysis of guilt over success miss Carrie's implicit critique of fame?

Carrie needed Marlene to acknowledge holes in her personality that fame could not fill. What threw Marlene off, partly, was that Carrie *did* enjoy the fame she fought so hard to achieve *and* needed Marlene to hear how badly she felt. Carrie needed Marlene's help on the way up, and now she needed it to face the misery success intensified.

As Carrie put it, no one wanted to pay attention to her shitty, yucky self. They only wanted the star to shine. Even Marlene listened to the negative just enough to soothe or rationalize it. Yes, Carrie poured a creative vein of self into starship. She believed in herself and what she expressed. What made her a star was something wonderful and real, moving and magical. But she was more than self shining on stage. There were excluded, neglected areas that would not go away. The more Carrie shone, the worse she felt.

First, fatigue. No one listened. Fatigue mounted, with insufficient results. Then colitis, which garnered some attention. Colitis mounted until it could not be ignored. Colitis became the inverse star of Carrie's life. Everything centred around it. She watched it constantly. She was proclaiming loud and clear that there was a sick nucleus as powerful or more so than her drive to be a star.

Marlene's panicky guilt and commitment to her work drove her to seek supervisory help outside the "system". I did not know Marlene or Carrie or anything about either of them, but I could feel the pull and power of the forces at work. Within moments I felt the impact of Marlene's anxious urge to make Carrie better and of her guilt over the down-spin. What once seemed a happy enabling was now tinged with dread. For the moment, I made room for dread.

Marlene began to feel relief. In supervision, akin to therapy, a therapist can voice anxiety, guilt, spin herself out, hear self more richly. "I pushed Carrie like her agent or husband. I got something out of her success. A little taste of refracted glory. I was terrified to hear Carrie's cries of weakness. I feared they'd never end. She'd never come back. She'd go to her weakest place and drown." There *are* people who drop through holes and never come back.

Marlene needed support with giving Carrie's dual tendencies their due. Individuals gravitate towards weak or mad or sick or wounded spots and need to touch the worst to feel real. Carrie failed to find a way to do this in tolerable doses and collapsed into illness. Her weakened, sick, mad, wounded body became a messenger of self. Individuals, also, gravitate to the best that is in them—strong points, gifts, talents. Carrie did this through acting. She funnelled messages of self through roles she played. Yet something short-circuited. Sometimes we pull ourselves together beyond capacity, beyond ability to find support. Some can take this for longer or shorter times. Carrie pushed past what she could manage.

Her integration ↔ disintegration rhythm was too one-way. There was overemphasis on integrating, too much stress on pouring everything into work and image, but not enough time to semi-collapse or fall apart and spontaneously come together throughout a day. Everything moved at higher speed and pressure, with little chance for aimless reverie. Too much focus, not enough blur.

The emphasis on turning out performances began to work against creativeness. Forced high-level behaviour replaced dream-time. She had to act before she was ready. Carrie's love of creativity partly fuelled her collapse. She was determined to maintain a high level of creativity in spite of daily pressure, at the same time as her creative self protested against abusive lack of dream-time.

Not everyone handles success badly. Carrie was a disaster waiting to happen. From an early age, she had been put down, made to feel bad about herself. She tried to make up for this by gravitating towards people who offered support. The latter usually came with a price. She learned to give herself up to others superficially while remaining deeply, invisibly defiant. Meanwhile, she cultivated her gifts.

Without quite realizing the extent of it, deep tensions were building within herself. On the one hand, she made people feel she trusted them and got what support she could. More deeply (usually rightly), she remained mistrustful and guarded, convinced that there was no one to rely on but herself. It was not that she was cut off and calculating, although that could be so. It was more that she remained somehow hidden, unaffected, left out, even as she moved ahead. She had no way of reconciling joy with blankness and deadness.

She clung to and milked gifted slivers of self, avoiding holes. She succeeded and so forgot weak and damaged areas, not wanting to be dragged down. Perhaps it was not fame that was deadening. Fame was thrilling. Perhaps its very excitement raised the level of deadness within. A higher intensity of life raised the level of what was missing. Filling what could be filled made Carrie's long-postponed appointment with missing and deformed areas of self and life compelling.

Success, fame, creative passion, weak and sick spots blend and shift in a complex way. Carrie's creative self drew nourishment from wounds, longing, sorrow, as well as strengths and joy. An alliance between missing, injured, deformed elements and creativity fed Carrie's work. Creativity moves between suffering and joy. Fame inflames suffering as well as joy.

However, success and fame have their own momentum. Money and recognition can release and debase. In Carrie's case, the pace, pressure, and radiance of success threatened the alliance of creative passion with weaker or mad elements of self. The creative self could not keep pace with success. It could not process links with weak and sick bits of self fast enough to meet demand. Fragile links between creative and disenfranchised elements of personality began to give way, undergo rapid disintegration.

The ghastly fact that Carrie's digestive/evacuative system started to undo itself spotlighted the possibility that psychic digestion was compromised. Experience no longer stuck to Carrie's insides or circulated through creativity. Experience was not being metabolized or channelled. Everything poured through her. She poured through herself. Therapy poured through and out too.

Carrie's parents mixed rage and neglect with pockets of adulation. Winds of worship momentarily soothed prolonged states of emotional injury. Carrie grew up bleeding inside—a maze of wounds intermittently filled with beatific moments. "I died every day, all through the day, for years. What stayed alive was burnt and tortured. But there were moments—beautiful, joyful moments."

Carrie grew up nourished/tormented by damaged bonds. Those she loved and who loved her damaged her as she was forming. Through it all, she contacted a creative spark that lifted and almost saved her. As she became successful, those closest to her inflamed the damage that fed her creativity—damage she longed to escape and that her creativity could not support any longer. She gravitated to those who tried to control her by mixing intimidation and adulation. She rebelled and "asserted" herself through self-injury. There was a damaged portion of being in which she could remain herself only by wounding herself, even if it meant physical destruction. Wounding herself and creative performing competed as means of self-expression. Pulls towards obliteration/radiance cancelled themselves out.

The new thing was that Marlene sought help for herself and for Carrie. It is difficult to overestimate the value of seeking help beyond one's limits. No one in Carrie's life had cared enough to do so before Marlene. Many people helped Carrie along the way. They helped the strong, talented Carrie, the Carrie who could act. They helped her over weak spots and low points, gave her encouragement, provided openings. Quiet self-deformation and the sense of being left out of her life made a low background noise, to be taken for granted and passed over. Carrie's body brought the whole show to a halt. Marlene passed the message on in order to gain the courage to listen.

Freud wrote about sexuality as the forbidden and focused on its mix with aggression. The forbidden continues today, although it changes forms. In Carrie's life, the forbidden includes yucky, messy, weak sides of self that get in the way of achievement, that spoil the desired image and ability of self. The forbidden includes everything that might be unsuccessful. Success equals fulfilment, and fulfilment is everything.

What sort of success is it when breakdown in functioning communicates something important about states of self? Perhaps Carrie and Marlene were on the brink of an achievement that was as important, if not more so, than conquest through career. Sick, deformed, excluded elements of personality were on the verge of linking with another mind and heart. A coupling with healing and generative possibilities was trying to form, if support was possible.

Social pressure was too much for Carrie and Marlene and threatened to blow an incipient generative link away. Marlene needed support to begin making room for her worries. Would Carrie sink forever? Is it too late? Will a death process prove too powerful? Will everything Carrie and Marlene worked for go up in smoke? Will they be able to take pressure from agents, husband, important people, Carrie's friends and relatives, Marlene's colleagues? What will happen if they no longer do well and stop impressing themselves and others?

For the first time in half a year, Marlene began to look forward to Carrie's sessions rather than dreading them. She could feel her body relax and open and felt rounder, fuller. She saw how pinched, strangulated Carrie had become and still saw her radiance. She was ready to let in whatever came. She felt like a therapist again.

With room to breathe, Carrie's sit-down strike may run its course.

* * *

To say that a therapist is a double agent is an oversimplification. Therapy makes room for all sorts of polarities and many-sidedness, all kinds of included/excluded aspects of self. Carrie's life may seem a caricature but is not as atypical as might be supposed. Therapy helps to balance one side of personality against another, helps rhythms to develop between swings of self-states. This is as true for therapist as for patient. If the former's flow becomes clogged or jammed or aborted, the patient may intensify ills in an attempt to get through. Sometimes nothing less than emergency triggers alarm.

In Sam's case, time may force an emergency. As he enters middle age, he begins to sense that time does pass, that he will continue to age and someday be old. Not even dedication to truth and beauty can stop the flow of time. It has taken all the days of youth and adulthood (does he yet believe he is adult?) for basic facts to start seeping in. Life with beautiful women who are truth to him is messy and problematic beyond belief. He still expects physical beauty to mediate truth and remains on the outskirts of what actual relationships require.

In a way, Sam's and Carrie's plights complement each other. Carrie breaks down to demonstrate self's messiness. Being a star is one thing, dealing with personality foundations another. Are both possible? Can they feed, enhance each other? Does Carrie's breakdown emphasize an ethical problem with fame? Is fame at the expense of foundational issues cruel and ruthless? The answer in Carrie's case is yes, too much so. She has to right the balance, find the pivot. Her personality refuses to keep filtering itself through too narrow a bottle-neck. She needs more room for the unwanted.

Sam insists that he does not expect relationships to be easy. He is ready for difficulty. His partners are not. And those who want to stick it out are not right enough. Somehow the ideal and real do not quite mesh—they almost do, but in the end their union falls apart. Life is a tantalizing failure. What we go through in therapy is not enough to wake him up, although it does a little. The shock of getting older may be an ally, even if he tries to find ways around it. Sooner or later, with time as leverage, therapy will help Sam to take the plunge.

Carrie and Sam have trouble fitting themselves into a form that works in real living. They try to exceed the pinch of natural limits, only to be thrown back and become more pinched. Yet little by little Sam is mellowing, opening, even if he is still a fierce warrior. With help, banging his head against internal barriers makes him more compassionate. With Marlene's help, Carrie finds more room for self in private being, as well as on stage (they *must* feed, as well as take away from each other!). The damaged self needs to be part of a worthwhile dream. Both Carrie and Sam continue to push their edges, but a sense of the materials with which they work gives them pause. A ghastly, indecipherable logic in lives makes us wonder, smile through tears, as we indefatigably tinker around.

CHAPTER TEN

Shivers

M y work as a patient is what made me an analyst. But
many factors went into making me a patient. I slept in a
crib in my parents' room until age five. From the earliest
age, I listened for sounds in the night. I have never stopped listening. Some of my earliest dreams were primal-scene dreams.

I hated the crib. It meant being a baby, held back, compressed,
imprisoned, suffocated. The crib played a role in my becoming a
sort of lifelong rebel. As a young adult, I could not be free enough.
I am lucky to be alive, given the crazy things I did to feel free. The
rock musician who wrecks his guitar makes me wonder if I have
spent my life, in part, breaking cribs (hopefully, only a partial
model of therapy). The sense of being compressed looking for
spaces to pour myself into never left.

When I was six, my parents bought a house, and I had a room of
my own. I still tried to hear what they were doing at night, but

having my own space was a blessing. My new neighbourhood had kids, and I played all the time. I have never needed much to be happy. Walking down a street, looking around, swinging my arms is enough to make me smile. I used to whistle while I walked, and now my older son hums and whistles a lot.

I did not understand school until university. Classes in elementary school were leaden. Listening to teachers felt like being in a soundproof chamber. No soul echoes. No flashes of mind. A lot of memorization of things that did not mean much to me. At university, things opened. I finally understood what was going on. I loved learning. I fell in love with James Joyce, Socrates, Kandinsky, Klee, Ormandy's Bach (my first real girlfriend took me to see the Philadelphia Orchestra a lot). I bought a motorcycle, got girls on the back, saw Miles Davis, Bird, Bud Powell. I could fly.

In high school I would play hooky sometimes and go hear big bands at the Palace. Playing in bands helped get me through. Music was real nourishment. It was something I could feel inside out, soak up through my pores, feel soul's porousness. Psychotherapy is musical. It lives by improvisations of spirit.

The movement from parents' room and from crib to a room of my own, from a lonely neighbourhood to an active one, from school to university are examples of living in a cocoon for long periods of time, followed by periods of rapid expansion. Similarly, my move from Passaic, New Jersey, to New York City. As a boy I could see Manhattan's skyscrapers from my block and thought: "I'm going to live there."

Making the move to Manhattan was not easy. It took several false starts. I rented a room and could not move into it. I could not tear myself from my parents' home and Passaic, even as I desperately wanted to. University was finished. Now was the moment of truth. I was too weak to make the move. Therapy demonstrated its practical power by enabling me to leave home to find my way.

During my first year of analysis (3 times a week) I read Jack Kerouac's *On the Road* and D. H. Lawrence's *The Plumed Serpent*, and I wanted therapy to help me go to Mexico and just live. It was like having a genie in my corner. Make a wish—boom, a new life materializes. My analyst was somewhat sceptical and hoped I would continue with him. But empowered by the therapy genie, I got on a bus and went off to Mexico, played in a band, wrote, followed the moment.

I became a believer in the primacy of ecstasy. I remember one morning on a hill looking down on an empty lot in San Francisco. I decided to stare at a tree in the middle of the lot and try as hard as I could not to become ecstatic. But the tree won, and, after a struggle, my heart burst with ecstasy. Such moments convinced me that primary emotional reality is orgasmic ecstasy.

Yet my raw naked self was also a ball of agony. My ugly agony did not fit San Francisco's beauty. I met many friendly people and was never at a loss for things to do. I had more friends in San Francisco than New York, yet my loneliness was more intense than ever. My loneliness did not fit the West Coast life I led. One day I got the idea that my loneliness fitted New York.

Perhaps I was latently too hostile or wretched for San Francisco. It was easier for me to be wretched in New York. I felt that New York could absorb my blackness better. New York was a better mirror of my ugly self. There was a better fit between inner and outer isolation, loneliness, rage, paranoia, depression, excitement. I began to feel emotionally confined in San Francisco. In New York I felt free to go as deeply as I dared into my personal prison. New York was a better place for a tormented, ecstatic soul.

I re-entered analysis (5 times a week) within a year of returning to New York and eventually sought refuge in the world of therapy—as practitioner and writer as well as patient. I began working with disturbed children in schools and camps, and in Blueberry— a treatment centre for schizophrenic children—I was actually called a therapist. I loved looking at and listening to Mira Rothenberg, the clinical heart of Blueberry. I felt her feelings, intuitions, gropings. I loved the immediacy of her work. We fought a lot, but when I was with her I felt the warmth and breath of a living soul. I was, at first, put off by the ego of Helmuth Gumprecht, Blueberry's intellectual guru, but thrilled to his talks and his belief in our patients. It is an attitude I felt at one with and one that has grown ever since.

For some time analysis continued to be a wish-fulfilling vehicle. I wanted more beautiful girls—analysis helped me to get them. I wanted to travel—analysis paved the way. I wanted to write— analysis encouraged me. I wanted to be me living the moment— and analysis said: "Let there be the living moment." The moment stretched into years. What I did not quite notice was that I was falling in love with analysis, and, as Roustang (1982) writes, analysis never lets go. I was hooked.

My analyst started to worry as I entered my late twenties. He feared that our work could go on forever without my piecing a life together. The living moment was not enough. He felt I should go for my Ph.D., get married, dig into something apart from my flowing psyche. I guess my love of or addiction to analysis began to bother him. I spoke in his tone of voice, used his locutions, smoked a pipe like he did, read the same books. Analysis was my life, and he was pushing me away. He reduced my sessions to 4, 3, 2 times a week.

Something was wrong. I was contracting rather than expanding. He had got me focused on him; now he feared it had gone too far. His own life fell apart. His marriage ended badly. He left the city for a university position. I was left hanging with a painfully ruptured bond. I hated him. I hated him as I hated my father, whom I loved so deeply too. I hated him for making promises he could not keep—also one of the reasons I hated my father. My analysis was repeating wounds of my life, broken promises, broken hearts, broken connections. As deep as I could go, the wound was there. It seemed that it had been there before time. And now time intensified it.

I started graduate school a year after my analyst left the city. Apparently I needed to lose him before starting to build a life. There a fellow student, Susan Mulliken, recommended me to her ex-husband, Richard Mulliken, who ran a training programme at New Hope Guild, a psychiatric clinic in Brooklyn. I took to it like a fish to water. More important than courses and supervision was the chance to be with patients in sessions. Sessions are holy. They convey a sense of the sacred. Sessions mediate the growth of souls. Being with patients in individual therapy changed my life. Session life was something I felt at home with, something I could feel from inside, connect with. It was like finding an atmosphere or medium I could live in. Being in sessions as an adult in my early thirties felt as natural and creative as being in bands when I was younger— something I could sink my soul into.

Socializing has always been difficult for me. I have had friends and close relationships. I have been OK when there is a feeling between another and myself, or a deeply shared interest. But much of social life occurs outside personal links, and I have suffered from fear of people in impersonal settings from an early age. Therapy provides a safe haven for being with another person. I *could* hide behind my therapy mask, but more often therapy is a vehicle for emotional exploration and very deep contact. Therapy exists to explore the nature of links and ruptures between people, and it can do so *in vivo* in raw yet graceful ways.

I feel lucky to have grown into therapy at a time when there was no rush to finish quickly, when therapy itself and what went on in it dictated its length. The New Hope Guild supported the relationship between therapist and patient, and there was no pressure to abort or warp it for extra-clinical reasons. My patients gave me a chance to learn what I could do, what *we* could do, what *can* be done. We stayed with each other long enough for me to begin appreciating and studying some of the psychosocial ingredients that constitute therapy, a bit like an artist learning about materials by using them, discovering what he/they can do, the ever undulating limits of the possible. I summarized basic aspects of my New Hope Guild work in a chapter entitled "Working with 'Unwanted' Patients" in *The Electrified Tightrope* (Eigen, 1993, pp. 25–41).

I stayed with my patients longer than my analyst stayed with me. I was trying to complete my analysis and heal myself through them. My analytic work was motivated by my need to repair my own broken analysis. It was, too, trying to mend the unmendable. My younger brother was killed by a truck when he was almost 11 and I was 21. My mother never fully recovered, and to say that I felt guilty does not even come close. I suspect I became an analyst in part to bring my brother back to life. This is one reason why I have been attracted to the impossible and worked so long with many given up on by others—the psychotic (*The Psychotic Core*, 1986), the unwanted, undeveloped, malignant, recalcitrant, or otherwise maimed self (*The Electrified Tightrope*, 1993), the dead (*Psychic Deadness*, 1996).

Some patients have stayed with me for more than two and three decades, and I have indeed witnessed the dead come alive, the blind see, the lame walk. These therapies take me to places I might otherwise not go—mute wounds accessible only by tears of awe and outrage. Life is miraculous. To our horror, miracles of destruction often prevail, but we grow more delicately alive trying to better the balance.

Books have been integral to my development. They open seas of experience beyond the confines of one's life that enable one to dig more deeply into the bit of life one lives. In high school I was blessed with three moments of real reading. The first happened when I had to stay after school for some infraction I do not remember. I was alone in a classroom reading Galsworthy's *Strife*, which suddenly came alive. I do not remember this play except for a fire that still burns in me. Perhaps the destructive fire united with unconscious images of eternal flame, hell, fury—the pulse, heat, and violence of life. Whatever it was, it was more real for a time than the drab teachers and walls surrounding me.

The second occurred when I was in my final year, confined to bed by bronchitis. I read Thackeray's *Vanity Fair*. Again, I remember little of this book except some descriptions of Becky Sharpe. What stays with me is the feel of another world, an imaginative reality more real than most people, a world I could lose myself in, better even than staring at the sky.

The veil dropped more compellingly the third time, later in my senior year. I went to Philadelphia with a friend. He was thinking of going to Temple University and I to the University of Pennsylvania. He fixed me up with a date who was pleasant enough, but nothing happened. At the end of the evening, he made out with his girl in her room, while I waited alone in the living-room. My hand fell on a book by e e cummings, and that was the end of me. My soul's jaw dropped. Words melted. Language was alive. Meaning danced everywhere. A bar between me and my insides dropped away. Wow! This was great! This was home! Unlike other books in high school, I can still quote lines from e e cummings.

Over the years, such moments link with each other and build momentum. At university James Joyce, Plato, and sex taught me that experience is infinite. I fell in love with the stream of consciousness, the Good, infinities of soul worlds—soul orgasms, body orgasms, mind orgasms, being orgasms. I have spent much of my life dumbfounded as the kaleidoscope of experience keeps turning. Now and then I try to do a bit of work with multiple realities that do and don't get along. Most often I am overcome with awe or laziness.

I hung on to readings in depth psychologies and mystical tradi-
tions as rafts in strange waters. I read Jung and Fromm before
Freud, although I read parts of Freud more intensely than ever
now. I read existential psychology and philosophy in my late twenties, although I was hit by novels by Gide and Camus in my late
teens. In my early thirties a paper by Searles (1961) meant a great
deal to me. I loved two papers by my major analyst (Elkin, 1958,
1972)—true affirmations of the human spirit. I began reading
Winnicott (1958, 1971, 1989) in my thirties and get even more from
him today. I have been reading Bion (1965, 1970) for more than
twenty years and Lacan almost as long and have been giving semi-
nars on Bion, Winnicott, and Lacan for many years. Kohut (1971)
helped me immensely after my analysis broke up. I always get
something from Melanie Klein (1946). Marion Milner (1957) helped
link my basic intuition with psychoanalysis, particularly passages
on symbolic life expressing facets of creative experiencing, including the orgasmic joy of creativeness. I summarize aspects of my
meetings with Milner, Winnicott, and Bion in the "Afterword" of
The Electrified Tightrope (1993) and Chapter 7 of *Psychic Deadness*
(1996).

For years I went over childhood traumas that mis-shaped me.
My mother went to work when I was about 8 months old, and the
maid we had was devastating. She would put cream on her pim-
ples, wrap herself in a sheet, then pretend to be a ghost and tell me
I would never see my parents again. When the doorbell rang, she
sometimes hid in the closet and took me with her. My parents did
not act on my complaints, and I felt a growing helpless fear/rage.

The trauma list for my father was endless. I was terrified of his
rageful outbursts. He drank a great deal during my childhood. At
the same time, he was fearfully overprotective. I fought for years to
get a bike, never got to go to sleep-away camp, was scarcely ever
allowed to go to public swimming pools. It was a nightmare. My
mother was a soft, kindly woman, and her basic good-heartedness
fooled me into thinking that she understood me. Both parents installed in me a sense of basic goodness, at enormous expense.

In my ongoing self-analysis, particularly with Winnicott's and
Bion's writings, I have tasted how frightened my mother was of me
as a baby. She has since verified that she was terrified (more than
normally) of injuring me as a baby. My experience with her when

I was a little older suggests that she did not know what to do with my aggression either, that she also feared being injured. A melding of panic/joy/goodness/destructiveness characterized the emotional air I breathed. I have had to work long and hard to become a little less afraid of myself and others and to find constructive uses of fear and anger.

After years of reciting permutations of my traumatic upbringing, I began losing interest in how hurt I was. The wound that never heals meets the fire that never goes out in never-ending ways. I became less interested in my past than with getting on with my life. Suffering, ecstasy, inspiration were facts. My history made me part of the human race. As time went on, I became more interested in what went on in therapy for its own sake, as a process of soul making. Therapy is not only a soul searchlight. Interactions between patient and therapist actually create being and new nuances of being.

Therapy is far more than rehashing the past, understanding patterns, freeing oneself from destructive tendencies, although all these may be important. Therapy is part of being and, as such, is ever created by being and creates being. The model of a high-velocity particle collider creating new particles is too narrow. A physicist—perhaps Eddington—said: "Something unknown is doing we don't know what." This applies to therapy too. Bion (1965, 1970; Eigen 1996, pp. 45–68) is especially helpful in keeping the unknown/unknowable open. What has not happened may be more interesting and helpful than what has happened. And what is happening may never have happened quite this way before. Whatever we know about therapy, there is more we do not know, more we have not begun to live.

We work on becoming better partners with our capacities. There is no end to opening. Patient and therapist are ever on the brink of opening with each other in fresh ways. Two people coming together to create being is not unique, but to set aside time specifically for this purpose is not usual. I originally entered therapy in pain, to strengthen myself, fulfil wishes. Now it is more thrilling to let therapy teach me what therapy can be.

I would not be able to continue to progress in therapeutic work without my interest in religion. Mystical experiences provide models for aspects of therapeutic processes, and therapeutic processes tie mystical experiences to real living. I have seen individuals lost in mystical experiencing without a clue to what they were doing to themselves and others. On the other hand, there are individuals so mired in the confines of a narrow therapy that they are blinded to the impact of the Infinite. In *Coming Through the Whirlwind* (1992), I depicted an individual dedicated to psychological truth at the expense of spirit and an individual dedicated to spirit at the expense of psychological issues. In *Reshaping the Self* (1995, pp. 191–192), I use the Job story as a frame for therapy. The intersection of the psychological and spiritual is important for us today. Each amplifies and strengthens the other. They evolve together.

I am not a scholar, a systematic reader, or follower of any school. I have loved aspects of most religions I have dipped into. In my twenties I nearly became a Catholic, but became ill during instruction and abandoned this idea as part of my recovery. St. Augustine and Meister Eckhart are among those who have had an enduring impact on me. I have been sustained by parts of Taoist writings for more than four decades. I enjoy Rumi and imagine myself a Sufi. My contacts with Buddhist and Hindu masters have been intriguing and worthwhile. The Bible and *siddur* have exercised my imagination since childhood.

One of my proudest moments was a *Simchas Torah* (the holiday of Torah joy), when the rabbi called me up for a blessing, then whispered in my ear, "You're a chasid!" We made a *L'chaim* together and danced like crazy. The chasidic movement originated in a joyous heart connection to God, although it can reinforce narrowly parochial elements in Judaism as well. Jewish prayer, song, stories touch my heart and energy centres.

I use Buddhism, in part, as a psychic cleansing system. Emptiness and selflessness act as antidotes to this or that version of self. People narrow, even destroy themselves, defending this or that identity. The "I'm right—you're wrong" structure produces nightmares. A good dose of Buddhism protects one against destructive self-definitions, nationally, racially, personally.

To say I am a Chasid in heart, a Buddhist in head would be too simple. But the neutrality of open awareness keeps one mindful that there is more to go, that more is going on than one may be imagining, that something is happening beyond the identities we have constituted for ourselves. If pain is real, so is the joyous light through and beyond pain. Can one stop working with walls of personality short of anything less? Going through the light whets an even deeper, fuller appetite.

I married for the first time in my mid-forties, and having a family has had an enormous impact on my work. First of all, the opening of my heart upon having children made me view my patients in a new light. I think my work was more strident and brittle before children. Caring for children made me care for my patients more. My capacity for love grew. I became, too, better able to appreciate the complexity of family life from a variety of perspectives: different parents (husband, wife), different children. I made peace with my own parents as well.

To really endure and make a go of family life involves dimensions of personal sacrifice not required by the single life. Either I would find ways of growing in order to help make things work or we were in trouble. The pressure put on personality by family life is mind-boggling. One is besieged by problems that cannot be solved, impossible demands by loved ones, differences in time worlds (the time worlds of infancy and childhood challenge normal adult living, and *vice versa*), new levels of pain through deeper bonds with those you most want to benefit but struggle with, and so on. I have grown more in my marriage than in any period since my early twenties.

Catholic and Buddhist writings have viewed married life as second-best. Marriage saps the strength and resolve necessary for spiritual development. Daily chores eat energy that might have been poured into prayer and meditation. Marriage is sacramental for the masses who cannot pursue God full-time. My experience has been the opposite. Marriage has acted as an accelerant for my spiritual as well as psychological growth. The Holy Spirit thrives on and nourishes the soul ground to bits and pieces by daily torments. Nowhere does the soul grow more through its own demise than in everyday clashes with those one loves.

To grow enough to encompass multiple antagonistic pressures with those one loves makes the idea of going beyond polarities more than an abstraction. The work in the trenches required on a persistent basis by family living has broadened my sense of what therapy does. It has made me far more respectful of what people actually achieve in the way of real living in spite of themselves. Work with patients and family living feed each other.

Today my patients inspire me. I am inspired by what they have gone through and what they must yet go through to work with themselves. Therapy helps to sensitize people to their lives in ways they missed or could not reach on their own. It helps people become more respectful of what is possible and fosters the capacity to be inspired by the lives they and others live. It helps the capacity for inspired living grow in less destructive ways.

We work with suffering, yet serve *jouissance* (Lacan, 1957, p. 323) We mediate *jouissance* for each other at the same time that life's pressures mutate us. We learn and keep on learning to work with our wondrous mutant selves. The work forces us to dig into experience and keep opening. We go ever deeper into the faith/despair helix and shiver as a mysterious joy ripples through the agonies we encompass, that encompass us.

Afterdream

The portrayals in this book involve a kind of dream-work growing within damaged bonds and expressing the psyche's attempts to undo damage or make the best of it. There is deep pain in this work and deeper joy. Dreaming threads its way from trauma to joy. Joy is part of wonder.

Trauma speaks in dreaming, and dreaming spins webs around trauma in order to digest it partially. The fact that dreaming does not stop means that we never give up on ourselves. It is necessary and useful to give up for a time and stop self-bashing. But, like ants and bees, we regroup and keep on coming. Dream-work incessantly signals states of self, often mangled, strangulated threads of being, dangers, obstacles, impossibilities—and refuses to stay still. Dream-work is in constant motion. It does not stop trying to digest the indigestible. It creates mixtures of honey and horror and vision.

If dream-work is puzzling, it reminds us that we are part of a puzzling existence, and attempts at solution may bring benefits but not "closure". We are open questions at the moment of death, a great inventor of dreams.

Death is terrifying but is bound to psychic damage. Psyche fuses death and damage. Death and damage are omnipresent irritants. We cannot do away with either. But we can be together in ways that mitigate the severity of the damage and even take some of the edge off death. We can dream each other in ways that embrace the sense that having insides is important, that we do live inside each other, that our capacity to feel each other and ourselves is worth the try.

Self is the greater filter. Self alone and self to self. Death is mediated through self, through damaged bonds that colour self. There is a sense that if we can undo damage, we can undo death. But we are happy to live, digest what we can, give something back, lifted by the astonishing hope that lines our joys.

REFERENCES

Bion, W. R. (1965). *Transformations*. London: Heinemann.

Bion, W. R. (1970). *Attention and Interpretation*. London: Tavistock.

Bion, W. R. (1991). *A Memoir of The Future*. London: Karnac.

Bion, W. R. (1992). *Cogitations* (ed. by Francesca Bion). London: Karnac.

Bollas, C. (1987). *The Shadow of the Object*. London: Free Association Books. New York: Columbia University Press.

Eigen, M. (1986). *The Psychotic Core*. Northvale, NJ: Jason Aronson.

Eigen, M. (1992). *Coming through the Whirlwind*. Wilmette, IL: Chiron.

Eigen, M. (1993). *The Electrified Tightrope* (ed. by A. Phillips). Northvale, NJ: Jason Aronson.

Eigen, M. (1995). *Reshaping the Self*. Madison, CT: Psychosocial Press/International Universities Press.

Eigen, M. (1996). *Psychic Deadness*. Northvale, NJ: Jason Aronson.

Eigen, M. (1998). *The Psychoanalytic Mystic*. Binghamton, NY: Esf Publications; London: Free Association Books.

Eigen, M. (1999). *Toxic Nourishment*. London: Karnac.

Elkin, H. (1958). On the origin of the self. *Psychoanalytic Review*, 45: 57–76.

Elkin, H. (1972). On selfhood and the development of ego structures in infancy. *Psychoanalytic Review*, 59: 389–416.

Freud, S. (1920g). Beyond the pleasure principle (pp. 1–64). *Standard Edition, 18.*

Grotstein, J. (1983). Who is the dreamer who dreams the dream and who is the dreamer who understands it? In: J. S. Grotstein (Ed.), *Do I Dare Disturb the Universe?* London: Karnac.

Grotstein, J. (1990a). Nothingness, meaninglessness, chaos and the "black hole". I: The importance of nothingness, meaninglessness and chaos in psychoanalysis. *Contemporary Psychoanalysis, 26:* 257–290.

Grotstein, J. (1990b). Nothingness, meaninglessness, and the "black hole". II. *Contemporary Psychoanalysis, 26:* 377–407.

Grotstein, J. (2000). *Who Is the Dreamer Who Dreams the Dream? A Study of Psychic Presences.* Hillsdale, NJ: Analytic Press.

Klein, M. (1946). Notes on some schizoid mechanisms. In: M. Klein, P. Heimann, S. Isaacs, & J. Riviere (Eds.), *Developments in Psycho-Analysis* (pp. 282–320). London: Hogarth, 1952.

Kohut, G. (1971). *The Analysis of the Self.* New York: International Universities Press.

Lacan, J. (1957). *Ecrits* (trans. A. Sheridan). New York: Norton.

Matte-Blanco, I. (1975). *The Unconscious as Infinite Sets.* London: Duckworth.

Matte-Blanco, I. (1988). *Thinking, Feeling, and Being.* London: Routledge.

Milner, M. (1957). *On Not Being Able to Paint.* New York: International Universities Press.

O'Shaughnessy, E. (1990). Can a liar be psychoanalysed? *International Journal of Psycho-Analysis, 71:* 187–195.

Paul, I. M. (1997). *Before We Were Young: An Exploration of Primordial States of Mind.* Binghamton, NY: Esf Publishers.

Roustang, F. (1982). *Psychoanalysis Never Lets Go.* Baltimore, MD: Johns Hopkins University Press.

Searles, H. F. (1961). Phases of patient–therapist interaction in the psychotherapy of chronic schizophrenia. In: *Collected Papers on Schizophrenia and Related Subjects* (pp. 521–559). New York: International Universities Press, 1965.

Tustin, F. (1981). *Autistic States in Children.* London: Routledge.

Winnicott, D. W. (1958). *Collected Papers: Through Paediatrics to Psycho-Analysis.* London: Tavistock; New York: Basic Books. [Reprinted as *Through Paediatrics to Psycho-Analysis.* London: Hogarth Press and the Institute of Psycho-Analysis, 1975; reprinted London: Karnac, 1992.]

Winnicott, D. W. (1960). Ego distortion in terms of True and False Self. In: *The Maturational Processes and th Facilitating Environment: Studies in the Theory of Emotional Development*. London: Hogarth Press & The Institute of Psycho-Analysis, 1965. New York: International Universities Press, 1965. [Reprinted London: Karnac, 1990.]

Winnicott, D. W. (1971). *Playing and Reality*. New York: Basic Books.

Winnicott, D. W. (1989). *Psychoanalytic Explorations* (ed. by C. Winnicott, R. Shepherd, & M. Davis). Cambridge, MA: Harvard University Press.

INDEX